Philosophical Logic

PRINCETON FOUNDATIONS OF CONTEMPORARY PHILOSOPHY

Scott Soames, *Series Editor*

PHILOSOPHICAL LOGIC

John P. Burgess

PRINCETON UNIVERSITY PRESS
PRINCETON AND OXFORD

Library of Congress Cataloging-in-Publication Data
Burgess, John P., 1948–
Philosophical logic / John P. Burgess.
p.   cm.   — (Princeton foundations of contemporary philosophy)
Includes bibliographical references and index.
ISBN 978-0-691-13789-6 (hardcover : alk. paper)
1. Logic. I. Title.
BC71.B89   2009   160—dc22   2008050131

British Library Cataloging-in-Publication Data is available

This book has been composed in Archer and Minion Pro

Printed on acid-free paper. ∞
press.princeton.edu

Printed in the United States of America
10 9 8 7 6 5 4 3 2 1

Contents

Preface

PHILOSOPHICAL LOGIC, in one of several senses of the term, is just the part of logic dealing with proposed extensions of or alternatives to classical logic. The aim of this book is to provide a foundation in philosophical logic in this sense, sufficient to equip the reader to follow basic applications in analytic philosophy, and to tackle if desired more advanced works. There can be no question of encyclopedic coverage, but the branches selected for treatment—what they are can be seen from the table of contents—are ones generally agreed to be central and important.

Volumes in this series are intended to provide short introductions to various fields of philosophy, and both the limitations of length and the orientation towards philosophically rather than technically minded readers have been taken seriously here. Limitations of space have enforced concision. Some previous acquaintance with logic has to be presupposed, though only as much as would be supplied by any good introductory textbook, and even of that a rapid review is undertaken in the first chapter. Some proofs are omitted—or as is said, making a virtue of necessity, are "left to the reader as exercises." Again for reasons of space, these are the *only* exercises: there are no end-of-chapter problem sets. More problems may be found, however, at http://press.princeton .edu/titles/9037.html.

Bibliography and history, either one of which could easily fill a volume twice the size of this one, are given limited space. There are suggestions for further readings at the ends of chapters. These include works of my own where certain topics are more fully treated, but special care has been taken to direct the reader to sources of "second opinions" in the case of those anti-classical logics with which I am not in sympathy (not that anyone could sympathize with all of them). As for history, the negative point goes almost without saying, that in an expository work like this the ideas presented are with few exceptions not original with the expositor. Positive attempts to trace the history of the subject do

not go beyond unsystematic remarks and the usual device of at-
tachment of personal names to various items of interest ("Adams
criterion," "Barcan formula").

Any work on the present topic, and especially any short work,
will have to draw a balance between philosophical and technical
aspects of the field, and no way of balancing the two will please
everyone. On the one hand, philosophical topics, such as the
metaphysics of modality, that are connected with but not centrally
part of logic, and that are slated for treatment in other volumes
of this series, will be treated only briefly here. So, too, will be issues of philosophy of logic, which is no more to be confused with
philosophical logic than is history of geology with historical geology. Philosophical logic is a branch of logic, a technical subject,
and there is no need to apologize if this book is more technical in
character than others in the series in which it appears.

On the other hand, the reader more interested in an overview
than an immersion in the subject can simply skip or defer reading technical proofs, which are set off from the main text, thus
extracting an even shorter book from this already short book.
Above all the temptation to include topics of great technical interest but doubtful philosophical relevance has been resisted. The
center of gravity of "philosophical logic" today lies in theoretical
computer science, but not the center of gravity of this book, which
is written with the needs in mind of students of philosophy and
philosophers who are not specialists in logic. Among the more
technically oriented a "logic" no longer means a theory about
which forms of argument are valid, but rather means any formalism, regardless of its intended applications, that resembles a logic
in this original sense enough to allow it to be usefully studied
by similar methods. In this book I unashamedly take seriously
philosophical questions of logic in the original sense (such as the
question which modal system gives the right account of the formal logic of modal notions, or whether relevantists were right in
claiming certain classical forms of argument invalid) in a way the
more technically oriented would regard as reactionary or quaint.

Acknowledgments

My PERSONAL DEBTS go far beyond the published literature cited in the references at the end of the volume. My first teacher of logic, the late Ivo Thomas, introduced me to the lore of temporal and modal logic, much of it at the time unpublished, almost before he taught me classical predicate logic. Colleagues, especially the late David Lewis, were over the years frequent sources of information and insights. Generations of students in my seminar "Heresies in Logic" have presented me with an opportunity to try out various approaches, and have caught errors in early drafts of material eventually adapted for incorporation into this book. To all these persons I am most grateful, as well as to Scott Soames for the invitation to contribute a volume to the present series. Stewart Shapiro and Kit Fine carefully read the whole manuscript, leading to many improvements. It was a pleasure to work again with Ian Malcolm and Jodi Beder, and also with Sara Lerner, in the production of this volume.

Philosophical Logic

CHAPTER ONE

Classical Logic

1.1 EXTRA-CLASSICAL LOGICS

What is philosophical logic? For the reader who has some acquaintance with classical or textbook logic—as it is assumed that readers here do—the question admits an easy answer. Philosophical logic as understood here is the part of logic dealing with what classical leaves out, or allegedly gets wrong.

Classical logic was originally created for the purpose of analyzing mathematical arguments. It has a vastly greater range than the traditional syllogistic logic it displaced, but still there are topics of great philosophical interest that classical logic neglects because they are not important in mathematics. In mathematics the facts never were and never will be, nor could they have been, other than as they are. Accordingly, classical logic generally neglects the distinctions of past and present and future, or of necessary and actual and possible.

Temporal and modal logic, the first nonclassical logics taken up in this book, aim to supply what classical logic thus omits. It is natural to take up temporal logic first (chapter 2) and modal logic afterwards (chapter 3), so that the treatment of the more obscure notions of possibility and necessity can be guided by the treatment of the clearer notions of past and future.

1.2 ANTI-CLASSICAL LOGICS

Since classical logic was designed for analyzing arguments in mathematics, which has many special features, it is not surprising to find it suggested that for the analysis of extra-mathematical arguments classical logic will require not just additions (as with temporal and modal logic) but amendments. One area where classical logic is widely held not to work outside mathematics is the theory of the conditional (chapter 4). But the more controversial proposed amendments to classical logic are those that suggest there is something wrong even with its treatment of its originally intended mathematical area of application.

Such criticisms are of two kinds. If we think of classical logic as attempting to describe explicitly the logic accepted implicitly by the mathematical community in its practice of giving proofs, then there are two quite different ways it might be criticized. It might be claimed to be an incorrect description of a correct practice or a correct description of an incorrect practice. In the former case, the critic's quarrel is directly with classical logicians; in the latter, with orthodox mathematicians, revision in whose practice is prescribed. Relevantistic logic (chapter 5) in its original form appeared to be a species of criticism of the first, descriptive kind. Intuitionistic logic (chapter 6) is the best-known species of the second, prescriptive kind.

1.3 PHILOSOPHICAL LOGIC *VERSUS* PHILOSOPHY OF LOGIC

Logic, whether classical or extra- or anti-classical, is concerned with form. (On this traditional view of the subject, the phrase "formal logic" is pleonasm and "informal logic" oxymoron.) An argument is *logically valid*, its conclusion is a *logical consequence* of its premises, its premises *logically imply* its conclusions—three ways of saying the same thing—if and only if the argument is an instance of a logically valid *form* of argument. In modern logic forms are represented using formulas. What the reader of an introductory textbook is introduced to—what it is assumed the reader of this book has been introduced to—is on the one hand the art of *formalizing* arguments, representing their forms using formulas, and on the other hand the science of evaluating arguments once formalized.

What logical forms *are*, and how they are related to linguistic forms, are deep and difficult questions not of philosophical logic but of philosophy *of* logic. They are questions about what logicians are doing when they are at work, not questions that have to be resolved before logicians get to work. Indeed, logicians never would get to work if they waited for consensus to be achieved on such questions.

Similarly for the question of what premises and conclusions *are*. Here they will be spoken of as sentences rather than "propositions." It will be left to be tacitly understood that in general it is only when taken in context that sentences are true or false, and that for sentences to count as "the same" for purposes of logical analysis in a given context they need not consist of exactly the same words in exactly the same order. With these understandings, the only difference between sentences and "propositions" of real importance for our purposes will be that sentences can change in truth value over time, whereas it is said that "propositions" cannot (so that when a sentence changes truth value over time it is by expressing different "propositions" at different times).

All branches of philosophical logic borrow heavily from classical logic. While some previous acquaintance with classical logic is assumed here, introductory textbooks differ greatly in their notation and terminology, and a rapid review of the basics is called for, if for no other reason than to fix the particular symbolism and vocabulary that will be used in *this* book. The remainder of this chapter is a bare summary statement of the most important definitions and results pertaining to classical sentential and predicate logic. The reader may skim it on first reading and refer back to it as needed.

1.4 CLASSICAL SENTENTIAL LOGIC: FORMULAS

At the level of sentential logic, formulas are built up from *sentence letters* $p_0, p_1, p_2, \ldots$, standing in the place of sentences not further analyzed, using *connectives* written $\neg$, $\wedge$, $\vee$, $\rightarrow$, and $\leftrightarrow$, pronounced "not," "and," "or," "if," and "if and only if" (henceforth abbreviated "iff"), but representing negation, conjunction, disjunction, the conditional, and the biconditional, however expressed. The sentence letters are the *atomic* formulas. If A is a formula, then $\neg A$ is a formula. If A and B are formulas, then $(A \wedge B)$ is a formula, and similarly for the other three connectives. (The

3

parentheses are to prevent ambiguities of grouping; in principle they should always be written, in practice they are not written when no ambiguity will result from omitting them.)

And those are *all* the formulas. And because those are all, in order to show that all formulas have some property, it is enough to show that atomic formulas have it, that if a formula has it, so does its negation, and that if two formulas have it, so does their conjunction, and similarly for the other connectives. This method of proof is called *induction on complexity*. One can also define a notion for all formulas by the similar method of *recursion on complexity*.

To give an example of formalization, consider the following argument, in words (1)–(2) and symbols (3)–(4):

(1) Portia didn't go without Queenie also going; and Portia went.

(2) Therefore, Queenie went.

(3) $\neg(p \wedge \neg q) \wedge p$

(4) q

When formalizing arguments, turning words into formulas, it is convenient to have as many connectives as possible available; but when proving results *about* formulas it is convenient to have as few as possible, since then in proofs and definitions by induction or recursion one has fewer cases to consider. One gets the best of both worlds if one considers only $\neg$ and $\wedge$, say, as *primitive* or part of the official notation, and the others as *defined*, or mere unofficial abbreviations: $A \vee B$ for $\neg(\neg A \wedge \neg B)$, $A \rightarrow B$ for $\neg A \vee B$, $A \leftrightarrow B$ for $(A \rightarrow B) \wedge (B \rightarrow A)$.

1.5 Classical Sentential Logic: Models

A form of argument is logically valid iff in any instance in which all the premises are true, the conclusion is true. Here instances of a form are what one obtains by putting specific sentences in for the sentence letters, to obtain specific premises and a specific conclusion that may be true or false. But it really does not matter what the sentences substituted *are*, or what they *mean*, but only whether they are *true*. For the connectives are *truth-functional*, meaning that the *truth value*, true or false, of a compound formed using one of them depends only on the truth values of the components from which it is formed. Thus the truth values of the instances of premise (3) and conclusion (4) depend only on the truth values of the sentences substituted for p and q, and not their meaning or identity. A *model* for (part or all of) classical sentential logic is just an assignment of truth values, conveniently represented by one for truth and zero for falsehood, to (some or all of) the sentence letters. Thus a model represents all that really matters for purposes of logical evaluation about an instance, so that in evaluating arguments it is not necessary to consider instances, but only models.

The extension of a model's assignment of truth values to all formulas (or if only some sentence letters have been assigned values, to all formulas in which only those sentence letters occur) is defined by recursion on complexity. The value of a negation is the opposite of the value of what is negated, and the value of a conjunction is the minimum of the values of what are conjoined. Writing $V \vDash A$ to indicate that model V makes formula A true, we have the following (wherein (7) and (8) follow from (5) and (6) and the definitions of $\vee$ and $\rightarrow$ in terms of $\neg$ and $\wedge$):

(5) $V \vDash \neg A$ iff   not $V \vDash A$

(6) $V \vDash A \wedge B$ iff $V \vDash A$ and $V \vDash B$

(7) $V \vDash A \vee B$ iff $V \vDash A$ or $V \vDash B$

(8) $V \vDash A \rightarrow B$ iff $V \vDash B$ if $V \vDash A$

The argument from premises $A_1, A_2, \ldots, A_n$ to conclusion B is valid, the conclusion is a consequence or implication of the premises, iff every model (for any part of the formal language large enough to include all the sentence letters occurring in the relevant formulas) that makes the premises true makes the conclusion true. There is a separate terminology for two "degenerate" cases. If no model makes all of $A_1, A_2, \ldots, A_n$ true, then they are called jointly *unsatisfiable*, and otherwise jointly *satisfiable* (with "jointly" superfluous when $n = 1$). Like the notion of consequence, the notion of satisfiability makes sense for infinite as well as finite sets. If every model makes B true, it is called *valid*, and otherwise *invalid*. Note that if one formula is the negation of another, one of the two will be valid iff the other is unsatisfiable, and satisfiable iff the other is invalid.

Actually, the general notions of consequence and unsatisfiability, at least for finite sets, can be reduced to the special case of validity of a *formula*, by considering the formulas

(9) $\neg(A_1 \wedge A_2 \wedge \ldots \wedge A_n \wedge \neg B)$
(10) $\neg(A_1 \wedge A_2 \wedge \ldots \wedge A_n)$

For the argument from the A_i to B is valid or invalid according as the formula (9), called its *leading principle*, is valid or invalid, and the A_i are satisfiable or unsatisfiable according as the formula (10) is invalid or valid. Two formulas A and B are *equivalent* iff each is a consequence of the other, or what comes to the same thing, iff the biconditional $A \leftrightarrow B$ is valid.

The valid formulas of classical sentential logic are called *tautologically* valid or simply *tautologies*; with other logics, *tautologies* mean not valid formulas of that logic but formulas of that logic that are substitution instances of valid formulas of classical sentential logic; *countertautologies* are formulas whose negations are tautologies. The term *tautological consequence* or *tautological implication* is used similarly.

1.6 CLASSICAL SENTENTIAL LOGIC: DECIDABILITY

When the intuitive but vague notion of "instance" is replaced by the technical but precise notion of "model," the need to check *infinitely* many cases is reduced to the need to check *finitely* many. In (3) and (4), for example, though there are infinitely many instances, or pairs of sentences that might be substituted for the sentence letters, there are only four models, or pairs of truth values that such sentences might have.

The result is that classical sentential logic is *decidable*. There is a *decision procedure* for validity, a mechanical procedure—a procedure such as in principle could be carried out by a computing machine—that will in all cases in a finite amount of time tell us whether a given formula is valid or invalid, satisfiable or unsatisfiable, namely, the procedure of checking systematically through

6

all possible models. (The method of truth tables expounded in most introductory textbooks is one way of displaying such a systematic check.) It is easily checked that the argument (3)–(4) is valid (though it represents a form of argument rejected both by relevantists and by intuitionists).

1.7 CLASSICAL PREDICATE LOGIC: FORMULAS

There are many arguments that cannot be represented in classical sentential logic, above all arguments that turn on *quantification*, on statements about *all* or *some*. Classical predicate logic provides the means to formalize such arguments.

The notion of *formula* for predicate logic is more complex than it was for sentential logic. The basic symbols include, to begin with, *predicate letters* of various kinds: one-place predicate letters $^1P_0, {}^1P_1, {}^1P_2, \ldots$, two-place predicate letters $^2P_0, {}^2P_1, {}^2P_2, \ldots$, and so on. There are also the *variables* $x_0, x_1, x_2, \ldots$, and an *atomic* formula now is a k-place predicate followed by k variables. Sometimes a special two-place predicate symbol $=$ for *identity* is included. It is written *between* its two variables (and its negation is abbreviated $\neq$). Formulas can be negated and conjoined as in sentential logic, but now a formula A can also be universally or existentially quantified with respect to any variable x_i, giving $\forall x_i A$ and $\exists x_i A$. However, just as disjunction was not really needed given negation and conjunction, so existential quantification is not really needed given negation and universal quantification, since $\exists x_i A$ can be taken to be an abbreviation for $\neg \forall x_i \neg A$.

To give an example, here is an argument and its formalization in classical predicate logic:

(11) All quarterlies are periodicals.
(12) Therefore, anyone who reads a quarterly reads a periodical.
(13) $\forall x(Qx \rightarrow Px)$
(14) $\forall y(\exists x(Qx \wedge Ryx) \rightarrow \exists x(Px \wedge Ryx))$

An important distinction, defined by recursion on complexity, is that between free and bound occurrences of a variable in a formula. All occurrences of variables in an atomic formula are free. The free occurrences of variables in the negation of a formula are those in the formula itself, and the free occurrences of variables in a conjunction of two formulas are those in the two formulas themselves. In a quantification $\forall x_i A$ on x_i the free occurrences of variables other than x_i are those in A, while all occurrences of x_i are bound rather than free. Formulas where every occurrence of every variable is bound are called *closed*; others, *open*. In a quantification $\forall y A$ on y, the free variables in A are said to be within the *scope* of the initial quantifier. We say y is *free for x in A* iff no free occurrence of x is within the scope of a quantification on y. In that case we write $A(y/x)$ for the result of replacing each free occurrence of x in A by y.

1.8 CLASSICAL PREDICATE LOGIC: MODELS

The notion of *model* for predicate logic, like the notion of formula, is more complex than it was for sentential logic. The idea is that no more matters for the truth values of premises and conclusion in any instance are what things are being spoken of, and which of the predicates substituted for the predicate letters are true of which of those things. What the predicates substituted for the predicate letters *are*, or what they *mean*, does not matter.

To specify a model U for (some or all of) the formal language of classical predicate logic we must specify its *universe* U, and also for (some or all of) the k-place predicate letters which things in U they are true of. This latter information can be represented in the form of a *denotation* function assigning as denotation to each one-place predicate letter ^1P_i a set $^1P_i{}^U$ of elements of U, assigning to each two-place predicate letter ^2P_i as denotation a set $^2P_i{}^U$ of pairs of elements of U, and so on. If identity is present, then $=^U$ is required to be the genuine identity relation on the universe U, which as a set of pairs is just $\{(u, u): u \in U\}$. Thus a model consists of a set of things and some distinguished relations among them (sets being counted as one-place relations, sets of pairs as two-place relations, and so on).

The notion of *truth* of a formula in a model for the formal language of classical predicate logic is also more complex. Its definition is one of the centerpieces of a good introductory course in logic, "Tarski's theory of truth." The notion of truth is applicable only to closed formulas, but to define it we must define a more general notion of *satisfaction* applicable to open formulas. Intuitively, a formula $A(y_1, \ldots, y_k)$ with no more than the k free variables displayed is satisfied by a k-tuple $(u_1, \ldots, u_k)$ of elements of U, or in symbols,

(15) $U \vDash A(y_1, \ldots, y_k) [u_1, \ldots, u_k]$

iff the formula A is true when each free variable y_i is taken to stand for the corresponding element u_i. Truth is then simply the special case $k = 0$ of satisfaction. For present purposes we can work with this intuitive understanding, and there will be no need to recall the full technical definition, but it may be said that where $A(x)$ has just the one free variable, the analogues of (6) and (7) read as follows:

(16) $U \vDash \forall x A(x)$ iff $U \vDash A(x)[u]$ for all u in U
(17) $U \vDash \exists x A(x)$ iff $U \vDash A(x)[u]$ for some u in U

An argument is valid, its conclusion is a consequence or implication of its premises, iff every model (of a large enough part of the formal language to include all the predicate letters occurring in the relevant formulas) that makes the premise true makes the conclusion true. The notions of (un)satisfiability for a set of formulas, and (in)validity for a single formula, and equivalence of two formulas can then be introduced just as in sentential logic. While all these notions, involving as they do the notion of truth, in the first instance make sense only for closed formulas, they can be extended to open formulas. Thus $A(x, y, z)$ is valid iff it is satisfied by every (u, v, w) in every model, and satisfiable iff it is satisfied by some (u, v, w) in some model, or equivalently, is valid iff its *universal closure* $\forall x \forall y \forall z A(x, y, z)$ is valid, and satisfiable iff its *existential closure* $\exists x \exists y \exists z A(x, y, z)$ is satisfiable.

It has been indicated above that no more matters for the truth of a closed formula in a model than what objects are in the domain of the model and what distinguished relations among them the predicates of the language denote. But in fact a great deal less matters. All that really matters is the *number* of elements in the domain of the model, and the *pattern* of distinguished relations among them. For if we replace a model by another with the same number of elements and the same pattern of distinguished relations—the technical expression is: with an *isomorphic* model—then exactly the same closed formulas will be true. For instance, suppose we have a language with two one-place predicates P and Q and one two-place predicate R, and a model M with universe {♠, ♥, ♦, ♣} and with the denotations of P and Q being {♠, ♥} and {♦, ♣}, and the denotation of R being {(♠, ♥), (♥, ♦), (♦, ♣)}. If we replace it by the model M' with universe {1, 2, 3, 4} and with the denotations of P and Q being {1, 2} and {3, 4} and the denotation of R being {(1, 2), (2, 3), (3, 4)}, then exactly the same closed formulas will be true. In practice there is no need to consider any but *mathematical* models, models whose universes consist of mathematical objects, since every model is isomorphic to one of these. (In principle there would be no need to consider any but models whose universes are subsets of the set of natural numbers, though this fact depends on the Löwenheim-Skolem theorem, a result usually not covered in introductory texts.)

1.9 CLASSICAL PREDICATE LOGIC: UNDECIDABILITY

According to *Church's theorem*, whose establishment is a major goal in intermediate-level textbooks, whereas for sentential logic there is a *decision procedure*, or method for *determining whether* a given formula is valid, for predicate logic there is none. Hence one looks for the next best thing, a *proof procedure*, or method for *demonstrating that* a given formula is valid, when it is.

Every introductory text presents some proof procedure or other, but hardly any two the same one, and there are several formats for proof procedures ("axiomatic," "natural deduction," "sequent calculus," "tableaux," "trees"), all quite different in appearance. Yet all styles have some features in common. With all, a *formal proof* or *demonstration* is some kind of finite array of symbols, and it is decidable whether or not a given finite array of symbols is a proof of a given formula.

The format of an *axiomatic*-style proof procedure, for instance, is as follows. Certain kinds of formulas are admitted as *axioms* and certain kinds of inferences from premise formulas to a conclusion formula are admitted as (*primitive*) *rules*. A proof (of a given formula) is a sequence of formulas (the last being the given formula) in which every formula or *step* either is an axiom or follows from earlier steps by a rule. In practice when proofs of this kind are presented, as they will be in later chapters, the steps are not just listed but annotated (using obvious abbreviations), with each step numbered on the left and marked on the right either as an axiom or as following from specified earlier steps by a specified rule.

For any style for proof procedure, a formula is *demonstrable* or a *theorem* iff there exists some formal proof or demonstration of it; otherwise it is *indemonstrable*. There are two related notions. Conclusion B is *deducible* from premises A_i iff the formula (9) is demonstrable, and the A_i are jointly *inconsistent* iff the formula (10) is demonstrable. We define B to be *deducible* from an infinite set iff it is deducible from some finite subset, and define an infinite set to be *inconsistent* iff some finite subset is.

And for any style of proof procedure, there are two results to be established for it, namely, that every demonstrable formula is valid and every valid formula is demonstrable. The task of establishing the first result, *soundness*, is generally tedious but routine. The second result, *completeness*, is another of the centerpieces of a good introductory course in logic, "Gödel's completeness theorem." Since the relationship of deducibility and consistency to demonstrability parallels the relationship of consequence and satisfiability to validity, the coincidence of validity with demonstrability yields the coincidence of the other *alethic* or truth-related notions, consequence and unsatisfiability, with their *apodictic* or proof-related counterparts, deducibility and inconsistency. (The coincidence of consequence and unsatisfiability with deducibility and inconsistency in the case of infinite sets of formulas depends on the compactness theorem, a result often not covered in introductory texts.)

1.10 FURTHER READING

The single greatest resource for our subject is the *Handbook of Philosophical Logic* (Gabbay & Guenthner, 1983–89). Despite the title, it is not a book—and certainly not one that would fit in your hand—but a four-volume encyclopedia. A vastly expanded second edition is projected to run to eighteen volumes; but much of the very substantial additional material is on the technical side of the subject. The first edition covers classical background (volume 1), extensions of classical logic (volume 2), alternatives to classical logic (volume 3), and applications (volume 4). The five nonclassical logics treated in this book are surveyed, along with many others there is no room for here, in the middle volumes. The fact that the classical background occupies a full quarter of the whole is some indication of its importance. Another useful general reference is Goble (2001).

Temporal Logic

2.1 REGIMENTATION

Consider the following argument:

(1) Publius will vote and Quintus will vote,
    but Publius will not vote when Quintus votes.
(2) Therefore, either Publius will vote and then Quintus,
    or Quintus will vote and then Publius.

The argument cannot be treated by classical sentential logic, since such a compound as "Publius will vote and *then* Quintus will vote" (or the reverse), unlike the simple "Publius will vote and Quintus will vote," is not truth-functional. The argument does not especially invite treatment by classical predicate logic, either, since it contains no overt quantification. Classical logic makes no direct provision for arguments turning on temporal considerations.

This surely is because classical logic was originally developed for use in analyzing mathematical arguments, and the world of mathematics is timeless. Yet mathematics can be applied to the world of physics, and classical predicate logic *can* after all, at the cost of some artificiality be applied to arguments like that from (1) to (2), by borrowing an idea from mathematical physics. Mathematical physics takes time to be another dimension, and describes events as being located "At temporal coordinate x_0" as well as "At spatial coordinates (x_1, x_2, x_3)." Borrowing this idea, one can formalize the argument from (1) to (2), not using an atomic sentence letter p or q for a tensed sentence "Publius is voting" or "Quintus is voting," which may be sometimes true and sometimes false, but rather using a one-place predicate letter Px or Qx for "Publius is voting at time x" or "Quintus is voting at time x," which may be true *of* some "times" and false *of* other "times." In addition one uses a two-place predicate symbol written $x < y$ for "time x is earlier than time y." Then (1) and (2) can be represented as follows (with x thought of as the present time):

(3) $\exists y(x < y \wedge Py) \wedge \exists y(x < y \wedge Qy) \wedge \neg\exists y(x < y \wedge Py \wedge Qy)$
(4) $\exists y(x < y \wedge Py \wedge \exists z(y < z \wedge Qz))$
$\vee \exists y(x < y \wedge Qy \wedge \exists z(y < z \wedge Pz))$

The pertinent part of the formal language of classical predicate logic is just the part containing the one-place predicate letters and $<$. This we may call the *regimented* language, "regimentation" being one word for formalization in classical predicate logic of prose that does not especially invite it. A model U for the regimented language will consist of a nonempty universe $|U|$ or U, a two-place relation on the universe $<^U$ or $\prec$, and subsets of the universe P^U, Q^U, R^U, ... , assigned to the one-place predicates by a denotation function. Intuitively, the elements of U represent times; $\prec$ represents the relation of earlier to later; P^U, Q^U, R^U, ... , represent the sets of times of which various predicates, formed by tacking on to the end of various sentences the phrase "at time x," are true, or equivalently, the sets of times at which the original sentences are true. If $A(x)$ is a formula with no free variable but x, then $U \vDash A[u]$ means that A is true when u is taken to be the *present* time. The information represented by the denotation function that assigns each predicate letter P_i a set P_i^U can more conveniently be represented in a single object, a *valuation* function V assigning each pair (i, u) consisting of a natural number and an element of U a value one for truth or zero for falsehood. One obtains V by letting $V(i, u) = 1$ or $V(i, u) = 0$ according as $u \in P_i^U$ or $u \notin P_i^U$. Given V, one can recover P_i^U as $\{u: V(i, u) = 1\}$. Thus a model for the regimented language can be taken to be just a triple $U = (U, \prec, V)$.

For example, if $A(x)$ and $B(x)$ are the formulas in (1) and (2), then $B(x)$ will be a consequence of $A(x)$ iff for every model U and every element u of its universe, if $U \vDash A[u]$ then $U \vDash B[u]$. This is the absolute notion, but there is also a relative notion. A set U together with a two-place relation $\prec$ on it is called a *frame*. Given a class $\mathbf{F}$ of frames, we say $B(x)$ is a consequence of $A(x)$ *relative to* $\mathbf{F}$ iff for every model U whose frame part $(U, \prec)$ belongs to $\mathbf{F}$, the condition that if $U \vDash A[u]$ then $U \vDash B[u]$ is fulfilled.

To consider consequence relative to the class **F** of frames with some special property, say the property called *totality*, the property that for any elements v and w of the universe we must have either $v \prec w$ or $v = w$ or $w \prec v$, is in effect to assume the time order has this property. An argument not valid without the assumption of the property may become so with the assumption. Indeed, in our present example, $B(x)$ is *not* a consequence of $A(x)$ relative to the class of *all* frames, but $B(x)$ *is* a consequence of $A(x)$ relative to the class of *total* frames.

> *Proof.* For the negative point, consider a model with a universe of just three times u, v, w, with v and w both later than u, but no other earlier-later relationships, and with P true only at v and Q true only at w. Then u satisfies $A(x)$ but not $B(x)$. For the positive point, if u satisfies $A(x)$, by the three clauses of that formula P is true at some v later than u, and Q is true at some w later than u, and we cannot have $v = w$. By totality, either v is earlier than w, in which case the first disjunct of $B(x)$ is satisfied by u, or w is earlier than v, in which case the second disjunct is.

The result here is typical. Most arguments turning on temporal distinctions will turn out, when formalized in the manner indicated, to be invalid as they stand—or to apply the principle of charity, valid only as an *enthymeme* with some assumptions or other about the special properties of the temporal order as unstated additional premises.

The question whether such an unstated premise is true would seem to be one for physics, not logic, to answer. The answers given by physicists to such questions have changed over the years. Classical physics assumed the time order to be total; relativistic physics merges space with time and does not assume the spacetime order to be total; the alternative assumptions of special relativity differ from those of general relativity; and physicists have yet to arrive at a final theory.

Then again, the literal truth of the additional premises as assumptions about physical time is not always relevant. In applications in theoretical computer science, time is often taken as a sequence of discrete stages of computation (first, second, third, and so on), ignoring as immaterial the fact that in the actual physical realization of the computation these steps are not instantaneous and time may elapse between them.

Yet again, the *whole* truth about the time order has not always been what was at issue. Philosophers have often tried to determine how much of the truth about the time order can be determined *a priori*, in advance of discoveries in empirical science (though a tendency in the past to declare to be *a priori* features of one day's physics destined to be rejected by the next day's physics ought to and to some degree has discouraged such efforts in more recent philosophy).

Logic takes no stand for or against various assumptions, but only lays out the options, indicating for the philosopher or computer scientist or physicist which arguments are valid without any special assumptions about the time order, and which are valid as enthymemes on which assumptions about the time order as unstated additional premises. This, then, is how, and in what sense, classical predicate logic can treat temporal distinctions.

2.2 AUTONOMY

The regimented approach is artificial inasmuch as English, like many other natural languages, *grammaticalizes* the most basic time distinctions, indicating futurity or pastness by changing the tense of the verb or inserting temporal auxiliary verbs (changing "Publius is voting" to "Publius will be voting," as in the first conjunct of (1)) rather than by any kind of overt quantification ("For some time later than the present, Publius votes then," as in the first conjunct of (3)). In place of such quantification over "times," the *autonomous* approach of *temporal* or *tense* logic uses non-truth-functional connectives F and P. Then premise and conclusion (1) and (2) of our example may be represented as follows:

(5) $Fp \land Fq \land \neg F(p \land q)$
(6) $F(p \land Fq) \lor F(q \land Fp)$

F and P may be pronounced "will" and "was" (or "it will be the case that" and "it was the case that"), but really symbolize futurity and pastness, however expressed. Two further temporal operators G and H may be taken as abbreviations for ¬F¬ and ¬P¬ and read "it is always going to be the case that" and "it has always been the case that," though it turns out to be convenient to think of G and H as primitive, and F and P as abbreviating ¬G¬ and ¬H¬.

If one has a formalization in this autonomous style, one can always get a formalization in regimented style by applying the *Meredith translation*, which turns a formula A of the autonomous language into a formula A^* of the regimented language with one free variable x_0, as follows:

(7) $p_i^* \quad = \quad P_i x_0$
(8) $(\neg A)^* \quad = \quad \neg A^*$
(9) $(A \wedge B)^* \quad = \quad (A^* \wedge B^*)$
(10) $(GA)^* \quad = \quad \forall x_1(x_0 < x_1 \rightarrow A^*\dagger)$
(11) $(HA)^* \quad = \quad \forall x_1(x_1 < x_0 \rightarrow A^*\dagger)$

The $A^*\dagger$ in (10) and (11) is the result of increasing by one the subscript of each variable in A^*. We then have the following (wherein $\equiv$ represents logical equivalence):

(12) $(FA)^* = (\neg G \neg A)^* = \neg \forall x_1(x_0 < x_1 \rightarrow \neg A^*\dagger)$
      $\equiv \exists x_1(x_0 < x_1 \wedge A^*\dagger)$
(13) $(PA)^* = (\neg H \neg A)^* = \neg \forall x_1(x_1 < x_0 \rightarrow \neg A^*\dagger)$
      $\equiv \exists x_1(x_1 < x_0 \wedge A^*\dagger)$

As the reader can verify, * applied to the autonomous formalization (5) and (6) yields the regimented formalization (3) and (4) (apart from the notational change of writing p and q for p_0 and p_1, and x and y for x_0 and x_1).

Every formula of temporal logic has a predicate logic translation, but not vice versa. Thus the regimented approach is of greater expressive power than the autonomous approach. So why bother with the latter at all? Among several answers, two stand out, one more influential with computer scientists, the other with philosophers. The first is that there is generally a trade-off in logic between expressive power and other desirable properties. (For instance, classical predicate logic has greater expressive power than classical sentential logic, but the former is undecidable, while the latter is decidable.) The second is that the grammar of temporal logic is closer to that of natural languages like English. The point is not that natural, ordinary language is good, while artificial, scientific language is bad, but that since both types of language are and for the foreseeable future will be in use, it is important to understand the relationship between the two, for which it is useful to have formal representations of both.

It may be mentioned also that the fact that we can express more in the regimented than the ordinary way of speaking and writing may not always be a plus. For the transition from the ordinary way of speaking, with its tense distinctions, to the novel regimented way of speaking, which effectively abolishes them, raises certain vexing philosophical questions. For instance, thinking in ordinary terms, I *am* and always *have been*, as long as I have existed, and am always *going to be*, as long as I exist, three-dimensional. When we switch over, we face a new question. Should I think of myself as timelessly being *four*-dimensional, having perhaps three-dimensional "time-slices" past and present and future; or should I think of myself as existing only in the present, and being three-dimensional, and merely having past and future "counterparts," also three-dimensional, who are not myself, but are connected to me in some special way as predecessors and successors?

Turning from the motivation to the development of autonomous temporal logic, the Meredith translation suggests a notion of model. Namely, we can just take as a model for the autonomous language a model $U = (U, \prec, V)$ for the regimented language. Intuitively we may think of the elements of U as being "times," or alternatively, temporary *states* of the world—or better, bearing in mind what was said in section 1.8 about there being no need to consider any but mathematical models, as being numbers or other mathematical objects *representing* times or states. (Thus 0 may represent the present time or state, -1 that of an hour ago, 1 that of an hour from now, and so on. Just as in mathematical physics or economics mathematical representations of particles or traders get *called* "particles" or "traders," so logicians tend to *call* the mathematical representatives of times or states or whatever "times" or "states" or whatever. This transfer of terminology

18

from represented to representatives is harmless, so long as it is recognized for what it is.) We may then think of the relation $\prec$ as representing the earlier-later relation on times, or alternatively the *relative futurity* relation "when u is present, v is future" on states, and think of the function V as representing at which times or in which states the various tensed sentences represented by the various sentence letters p_i are true.

We need a notion of a formula A of the autonomous language being true in the model U at a time or in a state u—in symbols, $U \vDash A[u]$—intuitively meaning being true if u is thought of as *present*. But such a notion is immediately supplied by the translation, for we can define $U \vDash A[u]$ to hold iff $U \vDash A^*(x_0)[u]$. It is both feasible and desirable, however, to define truth by a recursion on complexity in the autonomous language, independent of the translation, which can be done as follows:

(14)	$U \vDash p_i[u]$	iff	$V(i, u) = 1$
(15)	$U \vDash \neg A[u]$	iff	not $U \vDash A[u]$
(16)	$U \vDash (A \wedge B)[u]$	iff	$U \vDash A[u]$ and $U \vDash B[u]$
(17)	$U \vDash GA[u]$	iff	$U \vDash A[v]$ for all v with $u \prec v$
(18)	$U \vDash HA[u]$	iff	$U \vDash A[v]$ for all v with $v \prec u$
(19)	$U \vDash (A \vee B)[u]$	iff	$U \vDash A[u]$ or $U \vDash B[u]$
(20)	$U \vDash (A \to B)[u]$	iff	$U \vDash B[u]$ if $U \vDash A[u]$
(21)	$U \vDash FA[u]$	iff	$U \vDash A[v]$ for some v with $u \prec v$
(22)	$U \vDash PA[u]$	iff	$U \vDash A[v]$ for some v with $v \prec u$

As the reader can verify, (19)–(22) follow from (14)–(18) using the definitions of $\vee$ and $\to$ and F and P in terms of $\neg$ and $\wedge$ and G and H.

A formula B is *valid* with respect to a class of frames $\mathbf{F}$ iff for every model $U = (U, \prec, V)$ with $(U, \prec)$ in $\mathbf{F}$ and for every u in U, we have $U \vDash B[u]$, and *satisfiable* with respect to a class of frames $\mathbf{F}$ iff for some model $U = (U, \prec, V)$ with $(U, \prec)$ in $\mathbf{F}$ and for some u in U, we have $U \vDash B[u]$. A formula B is a *consequence* or *implication* of formula A (and the argument from A to B is *valid*) with respect to a class of frames $\mathbf{F}$ iff for every model $U = (U, \prec, V)$ with $(U, \prec)$ in $\mathbf{F}$ and for every u in U, if $U \vDash A[u]$ then $U \vDash B[u]$.

For example, the argument from (1) to (2) is valid for the class of total frames, but not for the class of all frames.

Such are the basic notions pertaining to what are called *Kripke models* (as adapted to temporal logic, topic of the present chapter; they were originally devised for modal logic, topic of the next chapter). In the literature, one often finds instead the phrase "Kripke semantics." Since "semantics" is a term already in use by linguists for a theory of meaning, it is important to note that Kripke models were not and are not intended to provide a theory of the meaning of tenses and temporal distinctions (or moods or modal distinctions) in natural languages like English. Indeed, models generally deliberately leave out meaning, retaining only what is really important for the determination of truth values. To avoid confusion, one could distinguish "*formal* semantics" or model theory from "*linguistic* semantics" or meaning theory; but it is best just to avoid "semantics" altogether.

The traditional main task of temporal logic, *Prior's project*, has been to understand how assumptions about the structure of time, expressed in the tenseless regimented language, with explicit quantification over "times" or "states," correspond to assumptions about the validity of various argument forms in the tensed autonomous language that do *not* involve such quantification. We have seen one example so far, that the assumption $\forall x \forall y (x < y \lor x = y \lor y < x)$ of totality for the structure of time yields the result that arguments of the form of the one from (1) to (2) are valid. We will see many other examples below.

2.3 THE MINIMAL TEMPORAL LOGIC: AXIOMS

Any proof procedure for classical predicate logic gives rise to a proof procedure of sorts for temporal logic, with a proof for a temporal formula A being simply a proof for its translation A^*. To be compatible with the spirit of the autonomous approach, however, we would want a proof procedure that avoids anything like overt mention of "times" or "states," a constraint obviously not fulfilled by proof procedures based on translation. In other proof procedures (quite fine ones if one's purposes are technical rather than philosophical) "indices" and "labels" creep in that are just "times" or "states" in transparent disguise. The one style of proof procedure freest of this tendency is the axiomatic, which for just this reason will be the only style considered here.

The *minimal* temporal logic L_0 has as axioms all formulas of the following forms:

(23) A, where A is any tautology
(24a) $G(A \rightarrow B) \rightarrow (GA \rightarrow GB)$
(24b) $H(A \rightarrow B) \rightarrow (HA \rightarrow HB)$
(25a) $A \rightarrow GPA$ (25b) $A \rightarrow HFA$

and as rules the following, known as *modus ponens* (MP) and *temporal generalization* (TG):

(26)   from $A \rightarrow B$ and A to infer B
(27a)   from A to infer GA (27b)   from A to infer HA

Note that in general A does *not* imply GA or HA. TG only allows one to infer GA or HA if A has been obtained *as a theorem of logic*. Intuitively, the justification for TG is that logic is eternal, that if a formula A is a law of logic, it must be true for all time.

The minimal tense logic is sound for the class F_0 of *all* frames. In every formal proof, every line, including the last, is valid or true at every state in every model. To establish this we must show that each axiom is true everywhere, and that for each rule, if the premises have this property, so does the conclusion. For the paired axioms and rules the demonstration is similar for the two items of each pair, and only the (a) version will be discussed here.

As for MP, first note that by (20), for each state in each model, if $A \rightarrow B$ and A are both true there, then B is true there. It then follows that if $A \rightarrow B$ and A are true everywhere, then B is true everywhere, as required. As for TG, if A is true everywhere, then for any state u in any Kripke model U and any state v with $u \prec v$, A is true at v. It follows that for any state u in any Kripke model U, GA is true at u, and GA is true everywhere as required.

As for (23), first note that by (15) and (19) we have

(28) $U \vDash (A \lor \neg A)[u]$ iff $U \vDash A[u]$ or not $U \vDash A[u]$

But the condition on the right-hand side of (28) is a tautology (in English) and hence always fulfilled, so $A \lor \neg A$ is true everywhere.   21

And similarly with any other tautology in place of $A \lor \neg A$. For (25a) we have the following:

(29) $U \vDash (A \to \mathsf{GP}A)[u]$ iff if $U \vDash A[u]$ then for every v with $u \prec v$ there is a w with $w \prec v$ such that $U \vDash A[w]$

But the condition on the right-hand side of (29) is fulfilled, simply taking $w = u$. (24a) is no more difficult, and is left to the reader.

2.4 The Minimal Temporal Logic: Rules

It is not quite trivial to remark that the class of theorems of $\mathbf{L}_0$ is closed under MP. If $A \to B$ has a proof and A has a proof, then B has a proof—namely, the result of stringing the proofs of $A \to B$ and A together, one after the other, and adding B as a last line, justified by MP. The same holds of TG for the same sort of reason. But the class of theorems is also closed under other rules that we have *not* taken as primitive, and it will be well to note some of these.

First, a *substitution instance* of a formula is the result of substituting formulas for its sentence letters. The class of theorems is closed under the rule of *substitution* (Sub):

(30) from A to infer any substitution instance A'

For all formulas of certain specified *forms* count as axioms, and making a substitution of formulas for sentence letters in a formula of a given form leaves a formula of that form. The rules have an analogous property, so performing the same substitution at every line of a proof whose last line is A still leaves us with a proof, now with last line A'.

Next we have the *rule of tautological consequence* (Taut):

(32) from $A_1, \dots, A_n$ to infer any tautological consequence B

For if $A_1, \dots, A_n$ have as a tautological consequence B, then the leading principle of the argument from the former to the latter, or equivalently the formula

(33) $A_1 \to (A_2 \to \dots \to (A_k \to B)\dots))$

22

is a tautology, and being a tautology, an axiom. Having also A_1 as a theorem, by a first application of MP we get

(34) $A_2 \to \dots \to (A_k \to B)\dots)$

and then by $k - 1$ more applications of modus ponens we get B.

Next, the *mirror image* or *reflection* of a formula is the result of replacing the future operator G by the past operator H and vice versa (so that F = ¬G¬ is replaced by P = ¬H¬ and vice versa). The class of theorems is thus closed under the rule of *mirror images* (Mirror):

(35) from A to infer its mirror image $A^\S$

For the mirror image of any axiom is again an axiom, and similarly for the primitive rules, so if the mirror-image transformation is applied to every line of a proof whose last line is A, the result is still a proof, now with last line $A^\S$.

Next, a *tense* is any sequence of operators G, H, F, P. The class of theorems is closed under *Becker's rule* (Becker):

(36) from $A \to B$ to infer $TA \to TB$ for any tense T

It is enough to prove it for the four cases T = G, T = H, T = F, T = P, for these can then be applied repeatedly. Because of the mirror-image symmetry, it is enough to prove the cases T = G and T = F. Supposing we have a proof of $A \to B$, we can get a proof of $GA \to GB$ by tacking on a few lines at the end, and a proof of $FA \to FB$ by tacking on a few more.

Proof. Here are the "few lines":

i	$A \to B$	Given
ii	$G(A \to B)$	i, TG
iii	$G(A \to B) \to (GA \to GB)$	Ax
iv	$GA \to GB$	ii, iii, MP
v	$\neg B \to \neg A$	i, Taut
vi	$G(\neg B \to \neg A)$	v, TG
vii	$G(\neg B \to \neg A) \to (G\neg B \to G\neg A)$	Ax
viii	$\neg G\neg A \to \neg G\neg B$ or $FA \to FB$	vi, vii, Taut

Next, let $C(A)$ (respectively, $C(B)$) be the result of substituting A (respectively, B) for p in some formula $C(p)$. (The letter C

23

is supposed to suggest "context.") Then the class of theorems is closed under the rule of *replacement* (Rep):

(37)   from $A \leftrightarrow B$ to infer $C(A) \leftrightarrow C(B)$

Immediate corollaries or special cases (also to be cited as Rep) are: from $A \leftrightarrow B$ and $C(A)$ to infer $C(B)$; if $A \leftrightarrow B$ is a tautology, from $C(A)$ to infer $C(B)$; from either of $C(A)$ and $C(\neg\neg A)$ to infer the other, or in other words, to insert or delete $\neg\neg$ anywhere in a formula. The proof is by induction on complexity, and a good illustration of that method.

> *Proof.* For the atomic case, if $C(p)$ is p, then $C(A) \leftrightarrow C(B)$ is $A \leftrightarrow B$ and is a theorem by hypothesis. If $C(p)$ is a different sentence letter q, then $C(A) \leftrightarrow C(B)$ is $q \leftrightarrow q$, which is a tautology (hence an axiom, hence a theorem). So the result holds in the atomic case. Now suppose that $C(p)$ is a negation, $\neg D(p)$, and that the result holds for $D(p)$. Then given that $A \leftrightarrow B$ is a theorem, it follows by supposition that $D(A) \leftrightarrow D(B)$ is a theorem, and from this it follows by Taut that $\neg D(A) \leftrightarrow \neg D(B)$ is a theorem; but this is $C(A) \leftrightarrow C(B)$. The conjunction case is similar, and is left to the reader. Now suppose $C(p) = TD(p)$, where T is any of G, F, H, P, and that the result holds for $D(p)$. Then given that $A \leftrightarrow B$ is a theorem, it follows by supposition that $D(A) \leftrightarrow D(B)$ and hence $D(A) \rightarrow D(B)$ and $D(B) \rightarrow D(A)$ are theorems, and from this it follows by Becker that $TD(A) \rightarrow TD(B)$ and $TD(B) \rightarrow TD(A)$ and hence $TD(A) \leftrightarrow TD(B)$ are theorems; but the last is $C(A) \leftrightarrow C(B)$.

Finally, if A is (or can be so abbreviated as to be) built up from sentence letters using $\neg$, $\wedge$, $\vee$, G, F, H, P, the *dual* of A is the result of switching $\wedge$ with $\vee$ and G with F and H with P. The class of theorems is closed under the rule of *duality* (Dual), wherein $B^* \rightarrow A^*$ may also be called the *dual* of $A \rightarrow B$:

(38)   from $A \rightarrow B$ to infer $B^* \rightarrow A^*$
       where A^* and B^* are the duals of A and B

> *Proof.* Given A with dual A^*, let A' be the result of substituting for each sentence letter p in A its negation $\neg p$. We

need the lemma that $A^* \leftrightarrow \neg A'$ is a theorem. The proof of the lemma, by induction on complexity, is left to the reader. Having the lemma, if $A \to B$ is a theorem, by Sub $A' \to B'$ is a theorem, and by Taut $\neg B' \to \neg A'$ is a theorem, while by the lemma $A^* \leftrightarrow \neg A'$ and $B^* \leftrightarrow \neg B'$ are theorems, so by Taut again $B^* \to A^*$ is a theorem.

By Mirror and Dual many important results will come in four versions (a), (b), (c), (d), featuring G, H, F, P respectively as the most conspicuous operator. Thus we have duals to axiom (25a,b) (which will be treated on a par with axioms in proofs):

(25c) $\mathsf{PG}A \to A$ (25d) $\mathsf{FH}A \to A$

Later we will consider extending $\mathbf{L}_0$ by adding axioms that are valid only for smaller subclasses of $\mathbf{F}_0$. The rules above depend only on the fact that certain axioms and rules are present in $\mathbf{L}_0$, and automatically hold for any extension, apart from Mirror, which will hold if (as will in fact be the case in the examples considered here) for every new axiom, its mirror image is either also taken as an axiom, or derived as a theorem.

2.5 THE MINIMAL TEMPORAL LOGIC: THEOREMS

We next note briefly some theorems obtainable from our axioms and rules. A first example is a pair of companions to axioms (24a,b):

(24c) $\mathsf{G}(A \to B) \to (\mathsf{F}A \to \mathsf{F}B)$
(24d) $\mathsf{H}(A \to B) \to (\mathsf{P}A \to \mathsf{P}B)$

Proof. Since these are mirror images it suffices to prove just one of them. The formula that abbreviates to (24c) may be proved as follows:

i	$(A \wedge B) \to A$	Ax
ii	$\mathsf{G}(A \wedge B) \to \mathsf{G}A$	i, Becker
iii	$(A \wedge B) \to B$	Ax
iv	$\mathsf{G}(A \wedge B) \to \mathsf{G}B$	iii, Becker
v	$\mathsf{G}(A \wedge B) \to (\mathsf{G}A \wedge \mathsf{G}B)$	ii, iv, Taut

vi	$(A \rightarrow B) \rightarrow (\neg B \rightarrow \neg A)$	Ax
vii	$G(A \rightarrow B) \rightarrow G(\neg B \rightarrow \neg A)$	vi, Becker
viii	$G(\neg B \rightarrow \neg A) \rightarrow (G\neg B \rightarrow G\neg A)$	Ax
ix	$G(A \rightarrow B) \rightarrow (\neg G\neg A \rightarrow \neg G\neg B)$	vii, viii, Taut

Another example:

(38a) $(GA_1 \wedge \ldots \wedge GA_n) \leftrightarrow G(A_1 \wedge \ldots \wedge A_n)$

(38b) $(FA_1 \vee \ldots \vee FA_n) \leftrightarrow F(A_1 \vee \ldots \vee A_n)$

Proof. Since these are duals, it suffices to prove just one of them. We do the case $n = 2$ of (38a). The general case is similar.

x	$A \rightarrow (B \rightarrow (A \wedge B))$	Ax
xi	$GA \rightarrow G(B \rightarrow (A \wedge B))$	x, Becker
xii	$G(B \rightarrow (A \wedge B)) \rightarrow (GB \rightarrow G(A \wedge B))$	Ax
xiii	$G(A \wedge B) \leftrightarrow (GA \wedge GB)$	v, xi, xii, Taut

Yet another example:

(39) $(GA_1 \wedge \ldots \wedge GA_n \wedge FB) \rightarrow F(A_1 \wedge \ldots \wedge A_n \wedge B)$

Proof. Again we do the case $n = 2$.

xiv	$G(B \rightarrow (A \wedge B)) \rightarrow (FB \rightarrow F(A \wedge B))$	Ax
xv	$(GA \wedge FB) \rightarrow F(A \wedge B)$	xi, xiv, Taut
xvi	$(GA \wedge GB \wedge FC) \rightarrow (G(A \wedge B) \wedge FC)$	xiii, Rep
xvii	$(G(A \wedge B) \wedge FC) \rightarrow F(A \wedge B \wedge C)$	xv, Sub
xviii	$(GA \wedge GB \wedge FC) \rightarrow F(A \wedge B \wedge C)$	xvi, xvii, Taut

Still yet another example (with its dual), whose proof is left to the reader:

(40a) $(GA_1 \vee \ldots \vee GA_n) \rightarrow G(A_1 \vee \ldots \vee A_n)$

(40b) $F(A_1 \wedge \ldots \wedge A_n) \rightarrow (FA_1 \wedge \ldots \wedge FA_n)$

2.6 Towards the Temporal Logic of Classical Physics: Axioms

Turning from the temporal logic of any conceivable time order to that of the actual physical time order, a complete answer to the question of the correct temporal logic even for classical physics, let alone post-classical physics, is beyond the scope of this book, but some significant steps towards an answer can be taken. First some terms for various properties the relation of a frame $(U, \prec)$ may or may not have. In each case it is understood that the property specified is to hold for *all u, v, w.*

(41)	*transitivity*	if $u \prec v$ and $v \prec w$, then $u \prec w$
(42)	*R-totality*	if $u \prec v$ and $u \prec w$, then $v \prec w$ or $v = w$ or $w \prec v$
(43)	*L-totality*	if $v \prec u$ and $w \prec u$, then $v \prec w$ or $v = w$ or $w \prec v$
(44)	*R-extendibility*	$u \prec t$ for some t
(44)	*L-extendibility*	$t \prec u$ for some t
(45)	*density*	if $u \prec v$, then $u \prec t$ and $t \prec v$ for some t

The most natural example of a frame $(U, \prec)$ with all these properties is the *real* frame where U is $\mathbb{R}$, the set of real numbers, and $\prec$ is $<^{\mathbb{R}}$, the usual order on those numbers. This frame represents time according to classical physics, which makes the study of the temporal logic that results when all the above properties are assumed of special interest. Another frame $(U, \prec)$ with all these properties is the *rational* frame, the frame where U is $\mathbb{Q}$, the set of rational numbers, and $\prec$ is $<^{\mathbb{Q}}$, the usual order on those numbers. There are subtle further properties beyond those listed above that distinguish the real from the rational frame, and sophisticated formulas of temporal logic that hold for the former but not the latter; but the matter is beyond the scope of the present work.

Now for axioms that hold for frames fulfilling one or another of the foregoing conditions. The following are valid for the class of transitive frames:

(46a)	$GA \rightarrow GGA$	(46b)	$HA \rightarrow HHA$
(46c)	$FFA \rightarrow FA$	(46d)	$PPA \rightarrow PA$

The proof is essentially the same for all four, so we may consider just the (a) version. Given any transitive Kripke model U, we must show that for any state u in U, (46a) is true at u. To show this it is enough to show that if GA is true at u, then GGA is true at u. The former condition means that A is true at v whenever $u \prec v$; the latter, that GA is true at v whenever $u \prec v$, or equivalently, that

27

A is true at w whenever $u \prec v$ and $v \prec w$. The former implies the latter, since by transitivity $u \prec v$ and $v \prec w$ implies $u \prec w$.

The most basic fact about (46a) is that its addition to the minimal temporal logic $\mathbf{L}_0$ yields (46d) as a theorem. Then by Dual we get (46c) and (46b). This is one case where we do not need to add the mirror image of an axiom *as an axiom*, since we get it *as a theorem*.

Proof.

i	$GPA \to GGPA$	Ax
ii	$A \to GPA$	Ax
iii	$A \to GGPA$	i, ii, Taut
iv	$PPA \to PPGGPA$	iii, Becker
v	$PGGPA \to GPA$	Ax
vi	$PPGGPA \to PGPA$	v, Becker
vii	$PGPA \to PA$	Ax
viii	$PPA \to PA$	iv, vi, vii, Taut

The following are valid for the classes of R- and L-total frames, respectively:

(47c) $(FA \wedge FB) \to (F(A \wedge FB) \vee F(A \wedge B) \vee F(FA \wedge B))$

(47d) $(PA \wedge PB) \to (P(A \wedge PB) \vee P(A \wedge B) \vee P(PA \wedge B))$

Indeed, (47c) is (a slight variant of) the leading principle of the argument from (5) to (6), which was proved to be valid for the class of total frames; but the proof only really used R-totality. L-totality yields (47d) in exactly the same way.

The following are valid for the classes of R- and L-extendible frames, respectively; they are *self-dual* and there are no distinct (c) and (d) versions:

(48a) $GA \to FA$ (48b) $HA \to PA$

Proof. We may consider just the (a) version. Given any R-extendible Kripke model U, to show that for any state u in U, (48a) is true at u, it is enough to show that if GA is true at u, then FA is true at u. The former condition means that A is true at *all* v with $u \prec v$; the latter, that A is true at *some* v with $u \prec v$. The former implies the latter provided there is at least one v with $u \prec v$, which is what R-extendibility says.

The following are valid for the class of dense frames:

(49a) $\mathsf{GG}A \to \mathsf{G}A$ (49b) $\mathsf{HH}A \to \mathsf{H}A$
(49c) $\mathsf{F}A \to \mathsf{FF}A$ (49d) $\mathsf{P}A \to \mathsf{PP}A$

Proof. We may consider just the (c) version. Given any dense Kripke model U, we must show that for any state u in U, (49c) is true at u. To show this it is enough to show that if $\mathsf{F}A$ is true at u, then $\mathsf{FF}A$ is true at u. The former condition means that there is some w with $u \prec w$ at which A is true; the latter, that there is some v with $u \prec v$ at which $\mathsf{F}A$ is true, or that there is some v with $u \prec v$ and some w with $v \prec w$ such that A is true at w. But this latter follows from the former by density.

The most basic fact about (49a) is that its addition to the minimal temporal logic $\mathbf{L}_0$ yields (49d) as a theorem. Then by Dual we get (49c) and (49b).

Proof.

i	$A \to \mathsf{GP}A$	Ax
ii	$\mathsf{P}A \to \mathsf{GPP}A$	i, Sub
iii	$\mathsf{GP}A \to \mathsf{GGPP}A$	ii, Becker
iv	$A \to \mathsf{GGPP}A$	i, iii, Taut
v	$\mathsf{P}A \to \mathsf{PGGPP}A$	iv, Becker
vi	$\mathsf{GG}A \to \mathsf{G}A$	Ax
vii	$\mathsf{GGPP}A \to \mathsf{GPP}A$	vi, Sub
viii	$\mathsf{PGGPP}A \to \mathsf{PGPP}A$	vii, Becker
ix	$\mathsf{PG}A \to A$	Ax
x	$\mathsf{PGPP}A \to \mathsf{PP}A$	ix, Sub
xi	$\mathsf{P}A \to \mathsf{PP}A$	v, viii, x, Taut

2.7 Towards the Temporal Logic of Classical Physics: Theorems

Let us next collect some theorems of the temporal logic $\mathbf{L}^*$ obtained by adding to the minimal temporal logic $\mathbf{L}_0$ the additional axioms (46)–(49), sound for the class $\mathbf{F}^*$ of frames with the additional properties (41)–(45). First a lemma:

(50a) $(GA \wedge A \wedge HA) \to GHA$
(50b) $(HA \wedge A \wedge GA) \to HGA$
(50c) $FPA \to (FA \vee A \vee PA)$
(50d) $PFA \to (PA \vee A \vee FA)$

Proof. Proofs now will be given only in outline. It will suffice to consider the (d) version. Let B be the following equivalent of the negation of the right-hand side of (50d): $H\neg A \wedge \neg A \wedge G\neg A$. It will be enough to get $\neg(PFA \wedge B)$, and since we have $B \to HFB$, enough to get $\neg(PFA \wedge HFB)$, and since we have $(PFA \wedge HFB) \to P(FA \wedge FB)$, enough to get $\neg P(FA \wedge FB)$, for which it is enough to get $\neg(FA \wedge FB)$. Using (47c), for this it will be enough to get $\neg F(A \wedge FB)$ and $\neg F(A \wedge B)$ and $\neg F(FA \wedge B)$, for which it is enough to get $\neg(A \wedge FB)$ and $\neg(A \wedge B)$ and $\neg(FA \wedge B)$. The last two of these three are trivial, since $\neg A$ and an equivalent of $\neg FA$ are conjuncts of B. As for the first of the three, the remaining conjunct of B is $H\neg A$, so we get $B \to H\neg A$ and $FB \to FH\neg A$. This together with $FH\neg A \to \neg A$, which we have, gives $\neg(A \wedge FB)$, to complete the proof.

Next, the converse:

(51a) $GHA \to (GA \wedge A \wedge HA)$
(51b) $HGA \to (HA \wedge A \wedge GA)$
(51c) $(FA \vee A \vee PA) \to FPA$
(51d) $(PA \vee A \vee FA) \to PFA$

Proof. It will suffice to consider the (d) version. It is enough to prove that each of the disjuncts on the left-hand side of (51d) implies PFA. For the first disjunct, we have $A \to HFA$, and hence $PA \to PHFA$. The new axiom gives $HFA \to PFA$, and hence $PHFA \to PPFA$. But we also have $PPFA \to PFA$, so we get $PA \to PFA$ as desired. For the second disjunct, we have $A \to HFA$. The new axiom gives us $HFA \to PFA$, so we get $A \to PFA$ as desired. For the third disjunct, we have $FA \to HFFA$, and we also have $FFA \to FA$, giving $HFFA \to HFA$, so we get $FA \to HFA$. The new axiom gives us $HFA \to PFA$, so we get $FA \to PFA$ as desired, to complete the proof.

Together (50) and (51) yield easy corollaries:

(52a) GHA ↔ (HA ∧ A ∧ GA)
(52b) HGA ↔ (HA ∧ A ∧ GA)
(52c) FPA ↔ (PA ∨ A ∨ FA)
(52d) PFA ↔ (PA ∨ A ∨ FA)
(53a) GHA ↔ HGA (53c) FPA ↔ PFA

There is also a related result:

(54a) FGA → GFA (54b) PHA → HPA

Proof. It will suffice to consider the (a) version. It will be
enough to prove ¬(FGA ∧ FG¬A), since this is equivalent
to the conditional we want. Now we have an axiom that
gives us (FGA ∧ FG¬A) → B, where B is the disjunction of
F(GA ∧ FG¬A) and F(GA ∧ G¬A) and F(FGA ∧ G¬A),
so it will be enough to get the negations of each of these
three. The first and third are just alike, and the second similar and slightly easier, so let us consider the first. We have by
axiom G¬A → F¬A, from which we get FG¬A → FF¬A,
and having FF¬A → F¬A, we thus get FG¬A → F¬A.
So we have (GA ∧ FG¬A) → (GA ∧ F¬A). But we have a
theorem (GA ∧ F¬A) → F(A ∧ ¬A). Since we have ¬(A ∧
¬A) and therefore ¬F(A ∧ ¬A), we get ¬(GA ∧ FG¬A)
and therefore ¬F(GA ∧ FG¬A), as desired.

We also have some easier theorems, some using more of the
new axioms than others.

(55a) GA ↔ GGA (55b) HA ↔ HHA
(55c) FA ↔ FFA (55d) PA ↔ PPA
(56a) GA → GPA (56b) HA → HFA
(56c) FHA → FA (56d) PGA → PA
(57a) PGA → GA (57b) FHA → HA
(57c) FA → HFA (57d) PA → GPA
(58a) GA → GFA (58b) HA → HPA
(58c) FGA → FA (58d) PHA → PA

Proof. It will suffice to consider the (a) versions. (55a) is
immediate from (46a) and (49a). For the others, we have

31

$A \rightarrow$ GPA, and this on the one hand gives G$A \rightarrow$ GGPA, while we also have GGP$A \rightarrow$ GPA, to give (56a), and on the other hand gives P$A \rightarrow$ GPPA, while we also have GPP$A \rightarrow$ GPA, to give (57d). (58a) is left to the reader.

2.8 REDUCTION OF TENSES

Now for an application of sorts. Temporal logic treats the temporal operators as iterable without limit; not so natural languages like English. One can form from the present "do" the past "did" and the past perfect "had done," a sort of double past, but any natural-language reading of something like PPPPp is clumsy. There is a result about L*, *Hamblin's theorem*, showing that most iterations collapse assuming classical physics—a fact that, one may speculate, perhaps suggests why natural language does not *need* to allow unlimited iteration.

The result in question says that for every "tense" or sequence of tense operators T, Tp is demonstrable in L* to be equivalent to Sp for some S from a certain list of fourteen "tenses" (or fifteen including the empty tense $\varnothing$ for which $\varnothing p$ is just p). These include two series of six, each implying the next, namely the past series FH, H, PH, HP, P, GP and the future series PG, G, FG, GF, F, HF, plus GH = HG, which implies them all, and FP = PF, which they all imply. The further implications that hold among these have been listed as theorems above.

The proof that every other tense is equivalent to one of these reduces, given that doubled operators are equivalent to single operators by (55), to showing that any three-operator tense XYZ with X $\neq$ Y and Y $\neq$ Z is equivalent to some two-operator tense; by mirror-image and duality considerations, it suffices to prove this in the case Z = G. (For instance, GPG is equivalent to G, since we have on the one hand PG$A \rightarrow A$ by [the dual of] an axiom and hence GPG$A \rightarrow$ GA by Becker, and on the other hand $A \rightarrow$ GPA by an axiom and hence G$A \rightarrow$ GPGA by Sub.) For each implication that does *not* hold, it is possible to exhibit a Kripke model based on the real frame where at time 0 the premise is true and the conclusion false. (For instance, in the model where

p is true just at times $-\frac{1}{2}, -\frac{1}{3}, -\frac{1}{4}, \ldots$, $\mathsf{HF}p$ is true at 0 but none of $\mathsf{H}p$ or p or $\mathsf{F}p$ is true.) Considerations of space preclude presentation of this whole body of material here.

2.9 QUANTIFIED TEMPORAL LOGIC

Though the questions of completeness and decidability for temporal sentential logic have not been broached—$\mathbf{L}_0$ *is* complete for $\mathbf{F}_0$, and $\mathbf{L}^*$ for $\mathbf{F}^*$, and both are decidable, and something will be said about the method of proof in section 3.7—it is time to move on and consider briefly temporal predicate logic. What is perhaps the most usual axiomatic proof procedure for classical predicate logic starts with all tautologies as axioms and modus ponens as rule, and adds two axioms and one rule, *universal generalization* (UG), for quantifiers, with two more axioms if identity is present, thus:

(59) $\forall x A \to A(y/x)$ provided y is free for x in A

(60) $\forall x(A \to B) \to (A \to \forall x B)$ provided x does not occur free in A

(61) from A to infer $\forall x A$

(62) $x = x$

(63) $x = y \to (A(x/z) \to A(y/z))$ provided x, y are free for z in A

If we try the experiment of combining the axiomatics of classical predicate logic with that of temporal sentential logic, some curious theorems result:

(64) $\mathsf{G}\forall x A \to \forall x \mathsf{G}A$ (65) $\forall x \mathsf{G}A \to \mathsf{G}\forall x A$

(66) $x = y \to \mathsf{G}\, x = y$ (67) $x \neq y \to \mathsf{G}\, x \neq y$

Here (64) and (65) are called the *converse* and *direct Barcan* formulas, respectively, while (66) and (67) are called the *permanence of identity and nonidentity*.

Proofs.

i $\forall x A \to A$ Ax

ii $\mathsf{G}\forall x A \to \mathsf{G}A$ i, Becker   33

iii	$\forall x(G\forall xA \rightarrow GA)$	ii, UG
iv	$\forall x(G\forall xA \rightarrow GA) \rightarrow (G\forall xA \rightarrow \forall xGA)$	Ax

(64) follows from iii and iv by MP.

v	$\forall xGA \rightarrow GA$	Ax
vi	$P\forall xGA \rightarrow PGA$	v, Becker
vii	$PGA \rightarrow A$	Ax
viii	$P\forall xGA \rightarrow A$	vi, vii, Taut
ix	$P\forall xGA \rightarrow \forall xA$	from viii as (64) from ii
x	$GP\forall xGA \rightarrow G\forall xA$	ix, Becker
xi	$\forall xGA \rightarrow GP\forall xGA$	Ax

(65) follows from x and xi by Taut.

xii	$x = x$	Ax
xiii	$G\,x = x$	xii, TG
xiv	$x = y \rightarrow (G\,x = x \rightarrow G\,x = y)$	Ax

(66) follows from xiii and xiv by Taut.

xv	$x = y \rightarrow H\,x = y$	66, Mirror
xvi	$P\,x \neq y \rightarrow x \neq y$	xv, Taut
xvii	$GP\,x \neq y \rightarrow G\,x \neq y$	xvi, Becker
xviii	$x \neq y \rightarrow GP\,x \neq y$	Ax

(67) follows from xvii and xviii by Taut.

Intuitively (66) and (67) are correct. Since everything is the same as itself at all times, if x and y are one and the same thing at any time, then that thing, the thing x alias y, can never at any time fail to be the same thing as itself, the thing y alias x; and so contrapositively, if x and y are two distinct things at any time, they cannot ever be one and the same thing at any time.

It should be noted that our formal language contains no analogues of proper names or definite descriptions in natural language, and that neither (66) nor (67) by itself implies anything about the status of identities or nonidentities linking proper names or definite descriptions or any expressions other than variables. Though the topic belongs to philosophy of language rather than philosophical logic, it may be mentioned that the generally accepted view today is that $a = b \rightarrow G\,a = b$ and $a \neq b \rightarrow$ $G\,a \neq b$ do hold when a and b are proper names, but in general fail when *a* and *b* are definite descriptions. But it cannot be emphasized strongly enough that the reason why these principles are accepted for proper names has nothing to do with the formal derivation of (66) and (67).

Rather, it is based on the intuition of what is called "rigidity," according to which, when using a proper name, the person (or place or thing) spoken of when speaking about the present is the very same person as the person spoken of when speaking about the future or past. It follows that if two names each denote the same person when speaking about the present, they each denote the same person when speaking about the future or past; and if they denote different persons when speaking of the present, they denote different persons when speaking of the future or past. By contrast, the denotation of definite descriptions is (in general) not rigid but flexible. Thus "the President of the United States" formerly denoted Bill Clinton, at the time of this writing denotes George W. Bush, and by the time this book is published will denote someone else.

Intuitively (64) is incorrect, as becomes clear if one takes for *A* something like "*x* exists." For any future time it will be the case that everything that will exist then will exist then, but it is not the case for everything that exists now that for any future time that thing will exist then. And similarly for (65). This book is being written during the first decade of the twenty-first century. Everything that exists now is always going to have existed in the first decade of the twenty-first century, but it is not the case that at every future time everything that exists then is going to have existed in the first decade of the twenty-first century. So our experiment of combining predicate and temporal logic has ended in failure, giving us intuitively incorrect theorems. Even the derivation of the intuitively desirable (66) and (67) seems a dubious accomplishment when one reflects that the same method of derivation equally yields the intuitively undesirable (64) and (65).

One response to this situation is to defend (64) and (65) by denying that anything ever really begins or ceases to be. When this appears to happen, as when an animal is born and lives for a while and dies, the appearance is an illusion. Really the animal existed before its birth and will exist after its death, though only as an

35

abstract entity. What is temporary is not its existence, but merely its flesh-and-blood concreteness. What is wrong with this reply is not that the metaphysical doctrine of *temporarily concrete entities* is silly (silly though it is). What is wrong is making logic depend on a metaphysical doctrine, and that would be wrong even if the doctrine were more sensible. Temporal logic ought rather to be able to offer physicists and metaphysicians alike *all* the options, so that adopting any particular doctrine, silly or sensible, would show up in the validity of some *additional* law, not part of the *minimal* logic.

Another response to the situation is to claim that (64) and (65) are true if instead of the usual "presentist" reading of ∃ as "there is" we adopt an alternate past-present-and-futurist or "eventualist" reading of ∃ as "there has been or is or is going to be." What is wrong with this reply is that it is irrelevant. The whole point of autonomous temporal logic is to take tense distinctions seriously, which in particular means taking seriously that the "is" in "there is" is in the *present* tense. Our experimental quantified temporal logic was intended as a logic of present-tense quantifiers, and their modification by past and future tense operators to form past and future quantifiers "there was" and "there will be." So even if, as the reply suggests, our experiment succeeds in achieving some *un*intended aim (which is as may be), it still fails to achieve its *intended* aim.

Where did the counterintuitive consequences come from? The answer is that the rationale for the rule TG, that whatever is true for purely logical reasons is eternally true, does not strictly speaking apply to open formulas, such as appear in proofs in predicate logic, since these strictly speaking are not true or false, but only satisfied or unsatisfied by various objects. (Eternal Logic teaches us that $\forall x \exists y (y = x)$, for instance, is true; but it cannot strictly speaking be said that for anything that exists, Eternal Logic teaches us that *it* satisfies $\exists y (y = x)$. For Eternal Logic does not know that *it* exists.) Now there are alternative axiomatic proof procedures for classical predicate logic that involve only closed formulas, so we could try a second experiment, combining these with the minimal temporal logic. Unfortunately, though the details are beyond the scope of this book, while the first experiment gave us theorems we did not want, it turns out that the second *fails* to give us some theorems we *do* want.

The situation is somewhat clarified by an extension of the notion of Kripke model to temporal predicate logic. Details are beyond the scope of this book, but in outline a model will now involve (i) a set T of times or states, (ii) a relation $\prec$ of earlier-later or relative futurity, (iii) a universe U of objects, (iv) for each t in T a subset U_t of U, the set of the objects existing at t, and (v) a specification for each one-place predicate letter P and each t in T and each u in U whether or not P is true of u at t, and similarly for many-place predicates.

Note that since some predicates, such as "the death of x is remembered" or "the birth of x is predicted" can be true of an object that did or will exist though it doesn't exist anymore or doesn't exist yet, a truth-value must be specified for P and u and t even if u is not in U_t. However, the quantifiers are understood as genuinely tensed, so in the quantifier clause of the definition of satisfaction and truth, $\forall x A x$ is true at t iff all u in U_t (*not*: all u in U) satisfy A at t, and $\exists x A x$ is true at t iff some u in U_t (*not*: some u in U) satisfies A at t. With these specifications it turns out, as the reader may verify, that the converse Barcan formula holds if we have $U_t \subseteq U_{t'}$ whenever $t \prec t'$ (so nothing ever *goes out of* existence), while the direct Barcan formula holds if we have $U_t \subseteq U_{t'}$ whenever $t' \prec t$ (so nothing ever *comes into* existence). These results highlight the intuitive absurdity of the Barcan formulas, but a perspicuous axiomatic proof procedure delivering as theorems just the closed formulas valid for this model theory is lacking.

There remains a further respect in which the situation as regards temporal predicate logic is unsatisfactory: the logic fails to express some significant time-related logical notions. One was hinted at with the mention of "eventualist" quantifiers above: there are forms of past (future) quantification that cannot be analyzed as a past-tense (future-tense) operator applied to a present-tense quantifier. For instance (adapting a well-known example of David Lewis) it is correct to say that there have been three English kings named Richard, though of no past time would it be correct to say that there were *then* three English kings named Richard. (The three Richards lived in different centuries.)

Another takes a bit longer to describe. In predicate logic a two-place predicate letter stands for an expression in English with two blanks that need to be filled up with singular terms or noun phrases to make a complete sentence, and temporal operators apply to predicate letters representing such expressions. But in English tense modifications apply to *verbs*, and a single predicate expression, such as "_____ is as rich as _____ is," may contain *two* verbs, independently modifiable for tense. The result is that there are distinctions in English that our formulas cannot represent, as with the following pair, of which one but not the other suggests that the lady is already at least half as rich as the gentleman is:

(68) After Quentin gives her half his money,
Priscilla will be at least as rich as he (then) will be.
(69) After Quentin gives her half his money,
Priscilla will be at least as rich as he (now) is.

This deficiency is easier to recognize than to repair. There remains a good deal of work, mathematical and philosophical, to be done before temporal predicate logic can be said to be in a satisfactory state, technically or intuitively.

2.10 FURTHER READING

The reader looking for a second opinion will not, in this case, find one in the *Handbook*, since the chapter there (Burgess, 1984a) is by the present author, but will find Benthem (1991) especially clear and concise. What the reader will find in both sources cited is a fuller treatment than in this chapter, covering proofs of completeness, taking up in more detail assumptions about the time order (discreteness as well as density, and the condition of continuity that distinguishes $\mathbb{R}$ from $\mathbb{Q}$), and introducing additional temporal operators, Hans Kamp's *since* and *until*, and more briefly *now* and *then*. (A completeness proof for since and until logic appears in Burgess (1982a), with another for *interval* rather than *instant* temporal logic in Burgess (1982b). The *decidability* of the temporal logic of R is proved in Burgess & Gurevich (1985). The temporal logic of special relativity is worked out in Goldblatt (1980).)

For the philosopher, the second of the three books on the topic by Arthur Prior (Prior, 1967), the founder of tense logic, is still indispensable. It among other things describes the history of the subject in its early days, when little was published, and also discusses nonstandard temporal logics (including one based on a nontransitive "east-west" conception of time), and time and existence and quantification. The great seventh chapter deals with classical arguments (going back to Aristotle and the Stoics, and continuing through medieval into modern times) about future contingents and logical fatalism, using the tools of modern modal and temporal logic. A more formal treatment of this topic is to be found in Burgess (1979) and Burgess (1980); see also Thomason (1984); the subject has since been pursued in a long series of publications by Alberto Zanardo. Another historical source still of interest is Pnueli (1977), which launched the application of temporal logic in computer science. For the linguistics of tense and the related category of *aspect*, see Comrie (1985) and Comrie (1976).

Modal Logic

3.1 MODAL VERSUS TEMPORAL

As temporal logic is concerned with the relationships among *was*
and *is* and *will be*, or past and present and future, so *modal* logic is
concerned with the relationships among *may be* and *is* and *must
be*, or possible and actual and necessary. Modal logic goes right
back to the beginnings of logic, with Aristotle—and doubt and
disagreement over it goes almost back to the beginning of logic
as well, with Aristotle's immediate successors Theophrastus and
Eudemus, who completely revised their teacher's theories.

On one point there has been general agreement since then:
the possibility of A is the non-necessity of the negation of A, and
the necessity of A is the impossibility of the negation of A, so that
if we write $\diamond$ for "possibly" and $\square$ for "necessarily," then $\diamond A$
amounts to $\neg\square\neg A$ and $\square A$ to $\neg\diamond\neg A$. Generally one thinks of
$\square$ as primitive and $\diamond$ as an abbreviation. The notion possibly-so-
possibly-not or $\diamond A \wedge \diamond\neg A$ is called "contingency."

English, like many other natural languages, grammaticalizes
the most basic modal distinctions just as it does the most basic
temporal distinctions. Parallels between modality and temporality can be seen by comparing such arguments as the following:

(1) She will become a psychotherapist without becoming a
    physician.
(2) She won't become a psychiatrist without becoming a
    physician.
(3) Therefore, she will become a psychotherapist without be-
    coming a psychiatrist.
(4) She could have become a psychotherapist without be-
    coming a physician.
(5) She couldn't have become a psychiatrist without becom-
    ing a physician.

(6) Therefore, she could have become a psychotherapist without becoming a psychiatrist.

As the argument (1)–(3) about futurity could be formalized with the F-operator, so the argument (4)–(6) about modality could be formalized with the $\Diamond$-operator:

(7) $F(p \wedge \neg q)$ (10) $\Diamond(p \wedge \neg q)$

(8) $\neg F(r \wedge \neg q)$ (11) $\neg\Diamond(r \wedge \neg q)$

(9) $F(p \wedge \neg r)$ (12) $\Diamond(p \wedge \neg r)$

3.2 KRIPKE MODELS

One thing the parallels suggest is a theory of models for modal logic, namely, the same Kripke models used for temporal logic. Technically, all that changes is that we are now defining truth in a Kripke model for modal rather than temporal formulas. The shortest way to state the definition of truth is this. First, associate with any modal formula A a temporal translation A', produced by replacing $\square$ by G (which results in replacing $\Diamond = \neg\square\neg$ by $F = \neg G\neg$, turning (10)–(12), for instance, into (7)–(9)). Second, for any modal formula A and any Kripke model $\mathbf{U} = (U, \prec, V)$ and any state u, define $\mathbf{U} \vDash A[u]$ iff $\mathbf{U} \vDash A'[u]$. If one wants a definition by recursion on complexity not dependent on translation, one can simply copy the clauses for sentence letters p and negation $\neg$ and conjunction $\wedge$ from the definition for temporal logic entirely unchanged, and add as clauses for $\square$ and the resulting clause for $\Diamond$ the translations of the clauses for G and F, thus:

(13) $\mathbf{U} \vDash \square A[u]$ iff $\mathbf{U} \vDash A[v]$ for all v with $u \prec v$

(14) $\mathbf{U} \vDash \Diamond A[u]$ iff $\mathbf{U} \vDash A[v]$ for some v with $u \prec v$

Intuitively, the understanding of what the components of a Kripke model represent also changes. The elements of the set U will be thought of now as being or representing not *temporary* states of the world, but *possible* states of the world. The relation $\prec$ will now be thought of as being or representing not relative-futurity or "when u is present, v is future," but *relative-possibility*, "if u is actual, v is possible." In a large part of the literature, what have here been called "possible states of the world" (mimicking the terminology "possible states of the system" from physics) are called "possible worlds." The phrase "world-states" is sometimes used as a compromise between these two terminologies.

The "worlds" terminology, unlike the "states" terminology, tends to carry the connotation that the possibilities being contemplated are *maximally specific*. Thus in some examples the only "states" that would need to be considered might be those in which a certain coin comes up heads and those in which that same coin comes up tails, while to each of these states would correspond a vast infinity of "worlds" differing in the conditions of coins other than the one in question as well as in an unlimited range of other respects. Since maximal specificity is often not needed, this difference of connotation is one reason to prefer the "states" to the "worlds" terminology.

Another reason is that the high-flying terminology of "worlds" tends to provoke philosophical puzzlement in ways the more pedestrian terminology of "states" does not. For example, there is no obvious absurdity in the assumption that the whole system of possible states of the world exists, and that when we speak of merely possible states of the world, what is merely possible is not the existence of the state, but rather the world's being in it. By contrast, the corresponding assumption that a whole system of merely possible worlds exists, which seems to imply that a whole population of merely possible people exist (since worlds tend to be full of people), can easily be made to seem absurd. For what is it to say that all these people are possible but not actual, except to say that there could have been such people but there aren't? But then if one says there are such merely possible people, one is saying that *there are things there aren't*. Well, perhaps this can be straightened out, but we don't need to attempt to do so if we stick with states and forget about worlds, as will be done here.

With the interpretation of the relation $\prec$ we come up against a limitation in the parallelism between temporal and modal. Disagreements in temporal logic, such as that between classical physics and relativistic physics, naturally present themselves as disagreements about the structure of the earlier-later or relative-futurity relation. Disagreements in modal logic, by contrast, by no means naturally present themselves as disagreements about the structure of a relative-possibility relation. If we have any intuitive notion of that relation at all, it is far less clear and distinct than our intuitive notion of the temporal earlier-later relation. Calling the modal relation "accessibility" makes the symbol $\prec$ easier to pronounce, but not easier to understand. Since intuition can use all the help it can get, it may be worthwhile to digress to describe an optional alternate route leading to Kripke models.

The starting point is the principle that *the aim in setting up a model theory is that the technical notion of truth in all models should agree with the intuitive notion of truth in all instances.* A model is supposed to represent everything about an instance that really matters for the truth of that instance. Now when we consider sentences with no modalities, such as

(15) $\neg p \wedge \neg q$

all that really matters is the truth value of the sentences substituted for the sentence letters. So as a model we may simply take a valuation function $V_\emptyset$ assigning each sentence letter a truth value. Call such a thing a 0-model.

When we come to sentences with modal operators but no modal operators inside modal operators, such as

(16) $\neg p \wedge q \wedge \Diamond(\neg p \wedge \neg q)$

it will now matter not only what combination of truth values for the sentences substituted for p and q actually *is* realized, but also which possibly *could be* realized. So for a model we will need something like a valuation function $V_\emptyset$ (giving the combination of truth values that is actual) and a set of various further valuations V_1, V_2, ... (giving the various further combinations that are possible). Call such an arrangement a 1-model.

When we come to sentences with modal operators inside modal operators but no modal operators inside modal operators inside modal operators, such as

(17) $p \wedge \neg q \wedge \Diamond(\neg p \wedge q \wedge \Diamond(\neg p \wedge \neg q))$

a little thought shows that we will need to replace each of the 0-models V_1, V_2, ... with a 1-model: V_1 with a 1-model consisting of V_1 and certain $V_{1,1}$, $V_{1,2}$, ... , and V_2 with a 1-model consisting

43

of V_2 and certain $V_{2,1}$, $V_{2,2}$, ... , and so on, so that we have altogether a 0-model $V_\emptyset$ associated with a set whose elements each consist of a further 0-model V_i associated with a set whose elements are yet further 0-models $V_{i,1}$, $V_{i,2}$, ... , which arrangement we may call a 2-model.

A formula like (17) will be true in the 2-model if there are some i and j such that (i) $V_{i,j}$ makes p false and q false, and so makes (15) true, while (ii) V_i makes p false but q true, and so makes $\neg p \wedge q$ true, so that the 1-model consisting of V_i and the various $V_{i,1}$, $V_{i,2}$, ... makes (16) true, while (iii) the original $V_\emptyset$ makes p true and q false and so makes $p \wedge \neg q$ true, so that the whole 2-model, consisting of $V_\emptyset$ and the various V_1, and $V_{1,1}$, $V_{1,2}$, ... , and V_2 and $V_{2,1}$, $V_{2,2}$, ... , and so on, makes (17) true. The reader may find it instructive to think through what would be a 3-model, and truth for a 3-model, with reference to an example such as this:

(18) $p \wedge q \wedge \Diamond(p \wedge \neg q \wedge \Diamond(\neg p \wedge q \wedge \Diamond(\neg p \wedge \neg q)))$

If we seek a notion of model that will work for *arbitrary* formulas, however deep the nesting of modalities, we will end up with a model consisting of a lot of valuation functions V_s, indexed by elements of the set Σ of finite sequences of positive integers. Whether V_s makes a formula without modalities true is determined in the ordinary way, but for modality we will have something different:

(19) V_s makes $\neg A$ true   iff V_s does not make A true
(20) V_s makes $A \wedge B$ true   iff V_s makes A true and B true
(21) V_s makes $\Diamond A$ true   iff some V_t with $s <_\Sigma t$ makes A true

Here we have written $<_\Sigma$ for the *immediate extension* relation, the relation that holds between s and t iff $t = s, k$ for some natural number k. (So $\emptyset <_\Sigma 1$ and $\emptyset <_\Sigma 2$, and so on, while $1 <_\Sigma 1, 1$ and $1 <_\Sigma 1, 2$, and so on.) It proves convenient to merge all the little one-place functions V_s assigning truth values to sentence letters into a single big two-place function V assigning truth values to pairs consisting of an element s of Σ and a sentence letter, thus:

44      $V(s, p_i) = V_s(p_i)$.

We obtain the notion of a Kripke model if we allow *any* frame $(U, \prec)$ and not just the special frame $(\Sigma, <_\Sigma)$ to provide indices. This (metaphysics-free) route to Kripke models may be closer to the route by which they were originally arrived at. The reader will have to judge how far, if at all, it improves our intuitive understanding of "accessibility."

3.3 TAXONOMY OF MODALITY

If the primary reason for interest in different temporal logics is the existence of differing opinions about one concept, physical time, the primary reason for interest in different modal logics may be the existence of differing concepts of necessity and possibility. And a primary source of confusion is that the differences among these differing concepts have often been overlooked, in part because very similar grammatical indications are used for quite different concepts. Linguists distinguish several kinds of modality, *dynamic* and *epistemic* and *deontic*. In speaking of past events and deeds, for instance, dynamic possibility concerns *what could potentially have been done*, while epistemic possibility concerns *what for all we know may actually have been done*, and deontic possibility concerns *what might permissibly have been done*.

Different logics may be appropriate to different senses of "necessary" and "possible," a phenomenon essentially without parallel in the temporal case. If we ask, for instance, whether p implies $\Diamond p$, or equivalently, whether $\Box p$ implies p, the answer depends on which kind of modality we have in mind. There is a clear "yes" for epistemic possibility (since what was actually done cannot be something we *know* was not done), while there is a clear "no" for deontic possibility (since what is actually done is often impermissible). It is generally agreed, however, even for deontic logic, at least that $\Box p$ implies $\Diamond p$ (though even this is not absolutely uncontroversial, since some have subscribed to the dubious metaethical doctrine that there can be genuine *conflicts of obligations*, and not just of *prima facie* obligations, but of all-things-considered obligations).

The corresponding questions for temporal logic, whether Gp implies Fp or Hp implies Pp, are controversial. Believers in a steady state theory, with no first or last time, accept the implications, while believers in a big bang/big crunch theory, with a first and a last time, reject them. There is a consensus, however, that p does *not* imply Fp or Pp, that what *is* need not ever be again or ever have been before (though even this is not absolutely uncontroversial, since some have subscribed to a fanciful cosmological doctrine of *eternal return*). In all this we have another respect in which the temporal/modal parallels are imperfect.

Adding to the complexity of the situation, the three kinds of modality identified so far are genera rather than species. In particular, under the genus of dynamic necessity we may distinguish the species of *physical* necessity, or what could not have been otherwise so long as the laws of nature remained the same, from *metaphysical* necessity, what could not have been otherwise no matter what. Also in this genus is *historical* necessity, or physical necessity given the facts about the course of history up to the present. (The philosophical and scientific issue of determinism is the issue whether every future occurrence is already historically necessary or not; but unfortunately discussion of the logic of this issue, which involves combinations of temporal and modal operators, is beyond the scope of this work.) Likewise, under the heading of epistemic necessity, pertaining to knowledge, there falls also *doxastic* necessity, pertaining to belief.

Besides this, there are types of modality, notably *logical* necessity and possibility, that do not fit comfortably under any of the linguists' classifications. A further complication is that many who have written of "logical" necessity have meant not necessity arising from pure logic, but necessity arising from logic plus definitions, *verbal* necessity or analyticity. And logical modality itself is a genus with two species. For classical predicate logic, the truth-related or alethic notion of *validity*, truth by virtue of logical form alone, and the proof-related or apodictic notion of *demonstrability*, provability by virtue of logical form alone, coincide. But even for classical predicate logic these two kinds of logical necessity are conceptually distinct, their coincidence being a major result. Some other logics lack sound and complete proof procedures, and for them validity and demonstrability diverge not only in intension but in extension, and so do the two correlative notions of logical possibility, *satisfiability* and *consistency*.

Demonstrability may plausibly be considered a species of epistemic necessity, and validity may arguably be considered a species of dynamic necessity; but validity must be clearly distinguished from other species, especially metaphysical necessity. The stock example used to distinguish the two is the composition of water. Is it *necessary* for water to be H_2O? It is not *logically* necessary that water is H_2O, since there is no internal logical self-contradiction in Dalton's theory that water is HO, or in the ancient theory that water is one of four or five elements. Indeed, that water is H_2O is neither logically necessary (in either sense, demonstrability or validity), nor analytic, nor knowable *a priori*; and for most of human history it was not known even *a posteriori*. For most of human history, for all anyone knew, water might have been an element; it was *epistemically* possible that water was something other than H_2O. It is *no longer* epistemically possible, but for metaphysical modality we can say something stronger. It not only *is* but *always has been* metaphysically necessary that water is H_2O. For water cannot be and never could have been anything other than the substance that it is, and that substance a compound whose molecules consist of two atoms of hydrogen and one atom of oxygen.

Given the dependence of what laws hold for modality on what sense of modality is at issue, one would expect the modern revival of modal logic to have begun by carefully distinguishing the different senses. Given the parallelism between modal and temporal notions, and the far greater intuitive clarity of the latter, one would expect temporal logic to have been developed first, and modal logic to have followed, guided by the analogy with temporal logic as far as it goes. Given how greatly model theory illuminates the significance of formulas in temporal logic, one would expect a modal model theory parallel to temporal model theory to have been developed early, and to have guided the choice of candidate modal axioms to be considered. But the historical development of a science is seldom rational. A half-century went by in modern modal logic before Kripke models for modal logic were introduced, and temporal logic only developed about the same period.

It was even later before modern modal logicians recognized the importance of distinguishing logical from metaphysical necessities—and this although something much like this distinction, under the labels "formal" and "material" necessity, had been made already by medieval logicians centuries earlier.

Part of the reason that philosophers in the last century were slow to recognize metaphysical necessity was doubtless because, wishing to avoid mysteries, they wished to trace the origin of all necessity to our concepts, as one arguably can do in the case of the logically necessary, the analytic, and the *a priori*, though not in the case of metaphysical necessity. In the case of metaphysical necessity the most that can plausibly be done in the way of tracing things back to our concepts would be to claim that it is part of our concept of water that it is a kind of substance, and part of our concept of a kind of substance that it has a certain composition (known or unknown), so that a substance that had a different composition could not count as *that* substance. From such a claim it would follow that our concepts are what make it to be the case that whatever composition water has, it has that composition necessarily (in the metaphysical sense that a substance with a different composition could not be water). But that water necessarily has the composition H_2O would at most be a consequence of this conceptual truth together with the nonconceptual (and historically rather recently discovered) truth that water has the composition H_2O.

3.4 THE MINIMAL MODAL LOGIC AND FIVE OTHERS

Turning to technical developments, all systems of modal logic to be considered here will be extensions of the *minimal modal logic* **K**, the analogue of the minimal temporal logic $\mathbf{L_0}$, which has as axioms all formulas of the following forms:

(22) A, where A is any tautology
(23) $\Box(A \rightarrow B) \rightarrow (\Box A \rightarrow \Box B)$

and as rules modus ponens (MP) and *necessitation* (Nec):

(24) from $A \rightarrow B$ and A to infer B
(25) from A to infer $\Box A$

The system **K** is sound for the class $\mathbf{F}_0$ of all frames. The class of theorems is closed under the following further rules:

(Nec*)   from $\neg A$ to infer $\neg\Diamond A$

(Sub)   from A to infer any substitution instance A'

(Taut)   from $A_1, \dots , A_n$ to infer any tautological consequence B

(Becker)   from $A \to B$ to infer $\triangle A \to \triangle B$ for any modality $\triangle$

(Rep)   from $A \leftrightarrow B$ to infer $C(A) \leftrightarrow C(B)$
           from $A \leftrightarrow B$ and $C(A)$ to infer $C(B)$
           if $A \leftrightarrow B$ is a tautology, from $C(A)$ to infer $C(B)$
           from either of $C(A)$ or $C(\neg\neg A)$ to infer the other
           (that is, to insert or delete $\neg\neg$ anywhere in a formula)

(Dual)   from $A \to B$ to infer $B^* \to A^*$
           where A^* and B^* are the duals of A and B

Here in Becker's rule a *modality* is a sequence of $\Box$s and $\Diamond$s, while in Dual the dual of a formula built up from atomic formulas using $\neg, \vee, \wedge, \Box, \Diamond$ is the result of switching $\vee$ with $\wedge$ and $\Box$ with $\Diamond$. The theorems of the minimal modal logic **K** include the following:

(26) $(\Box A_1 \wedge \dots \wedge \Box A_n) \leftrightarrow \Box (A_1 \wedge \dots \wedge A_n)$

(26*) $(\Diamond A_1 \vee \dots \vee \Diamond A_n) \leftrightarrow \Diamond (A_1 \vee \dots \vee A_n)$

(27) $(\Box A_1 \wedge \dots \wedge \Box A_n \wedge \Diamond B) \to \Diamond(A_1 \wedge \dots \wedge A_n \wedge B)$

(28) $(\Box A_1 \vee \dots \vee \Box A_n) \to \Box (A_1 \vee \dots \vee A_n)$

(28*) $\Diamond(A_1 \wedge \dots \wedge A_n) \to (\Diamond A_1 \wedge \dots \wedge \Diamond A_n)$

The abbreviation $p \Rightarrow q$ is sometimes used for the "strict conditional" $\Box(p \to q)$. One consequence of (26) is that $(p \Rightarrow q) \wedge (q \Rightarrow p)$ is provably equivalent to $\Box(p \leftrightarrow q)$, and the symbol $p \Leftrightarrow q$ may be used indifferently as an abbreviation for either. All these results can be obtained by the same methods as were used for temporal logic in sections 2.4 and 2.5; indeed, they essentially *have been* obtained, as the reader can verify, though in a different notation, in those sections.

Now for stronger systems than **K**. The list of additional conditions on frames of interest in connection with modal logic is a bit different from that of interest in connection with temporal logic. In each case it is understood that the property specified is to hold for *all u, v, w.*

(29)	*reflexivity*	$u \prec u$
(30)	*transitivity*	if $u \prec v$ and $v \prec w$, then $u \prec w$
(31)	*R-convergence*	if $u \prec v$ and $u \prec w$, then $v \prec t$ and $w \prec t$ for some t
(32)	*R-totality*	if $u \prec v$ and $u \prec w$, then $v \prec w$ or $w \prec v$
(33)	*symmetry*	$u \prec v$ then $v \prec u$

The corresponding axioms (with duals of three) are as follows:

(34)	$\Box A \to A$	(34*)	$A \to \Diamond A$
(35)	$\Box A \to \Box\Box A$	(35*)	$\Diamond\Diamond A \to \Diamond A$
(36)	$\Diamond\Box A \to \Box\Diamond A$		
(37)	$(\Diamond A \wedge \Diamond B) \to (\Diamond(A \wedge \Diamond B) \vee \Diamond(B \wedge \Diamond A))$		
(38)	$A \to \Box\Diamond A$	(38*)	$\Diamond\Box A \to A$

What is probably the most important series of increasingly strong modal logics is the following:

(39)	**T**	=	**K** + (34)
(40)	**S4**	=	**T** + (35)
(41)	**S4.2**	=	**S4** + (36)
(42)	**S4.3**	=	**S4** + (37)
(43)	**S5**	=	**S4** + (38)

It can be established that (36) is a theorem of **S4.3** in much the same way that the corresponding result for temporal logic was established in section 2.7. It can also be shown that (37) is a theorem of **S5**, though we leave the proof to the reader.

Some traces of the irrational historical development of modal logic (the late arrival of model theory) appear in the nomenclature. As may be guessed, modal logicians once studied a series of increasingly strong modal axioms systems bearing the names **S1, S2, S3, S4, S5**. After the introduction of Kripke models, it was found that the first three systems corresponded to no important classes of frames, while a system intermediate between **S2** and **S4** but incomparable with **S3** and therefore ineligible for a name in the S-series did correspond to a very important class, as did two from among the several systems that had been interpolated as afterthoughts between **S4** and **S5**. There have been proposals to rationalize the modal notation, ignoring history, just as there have been proposals to rationalize English spelling, ignoring etymology. In both cases the weight of tradition has tended to prevail against such proposals.

T is sound for the class of reflexive frames; **S4** for the class of reflexive and transitive frames; **S4.2** for the class of reflexive, transitive, and R-convergent frames; **S4.3** for the class of reflexive, transitive, and R-total frames; and **S5** for the class of reflexive, symmetric, and transitive frames. (A relation that is reflexive, symmetric, and transitive is called an *equivalence relation*.) To show all this it is enough to show the five special axioms of the various systems are valid for the indicated classes of frames.

Proofs. (34) is valid for the class of reflexive frames. For if $\Box A$ is true at u, then A is true at every v with $u \prec v$, and by reflexivity this includes u itself, so A is true at u.

(36) is valid for the class of R-convergent frames. For if $\Diamond \Box A$ is true at u, then $\Box A$ is true at some v with $u \prec v$. Then given any w with $u \prec w$, by R-convergence there must be a t with $v \prec t$ and $w \prec t$. Since $v \prec t$ and $\Box A$ is true at v, p is true at t, and since $w \prec t$, $\Diamond A$ is true at w. Since this is so for *any* w with $u \prec w$, $\Box \Diamond A$ is true at u.

(38) is valid for the class of symmetric frames. For if A is true at u, then for every v with $u \prec v$ there is a w with $v \prec w$ such that A is true at w, namely, $w = u$ itself, since we will have $v \prec u$ by symmetry. It follows that $\Diamond A$ is true at v, and since this is so for any v with $u \prec v$, $\Box \Diamond A$ is true at u. (It follows that the system $\mathbf{B} = \mathbf{T} + (38)$ is sound for the class of reflexive and symmetric frames.)

It can be established that (35) is valid for the class of transitive frames much as the corresponding result for temporal logic was established in section 2.6. It can be established that (37) is valid for the class of reflexive R-total frames much as the corresponding result for temporal logic was established in section 2.7.

Two alternates to definitions (42) and (43) are worthy of note. The same set of theorems is obtained if we replace axiom (37) of **S4.3** by the following:

(44) $\Box(\Box A \to B) \lor \Box(\Box B \to A)$

The same set of theorems is obtained if we replace axioms (35) and (38) of **S5** by the following:

(45) $\Diamond A \to \Box \Diamond A$

Proofs. Given (37), let $C = \Box A \land \neg B$ and $D = \Box B \land \neg A$. By (26*), $\Diamond C$ implies $\Diamond \neg B$ or equivalently $\neg \Box B$, and similarly $\Diamond D$ implies $\neg \Box A$. It follows that $\neg(C \land \Diamond D)$ and $\neg(D \land \Diamond C)$ are theorems of **K**, hence so are $\neg \Diamond(C \land \Diamond D)$ and $\neg \Diamond(D \land \Diamond C)$. But then (37) yields $\neg(\Diamond C \land \Diamond D)$, or equivalently $\Box \neg C \lor \Box \neg D$, and this is equivalent to (44).

Conversely, given (44), let $C = \neg \Diamond(A \land \Diamond B)$ and $D = \neg \Diamond(B \land \Diamond A)$, while $E = \Box(\Box \neg A \to \neg B)$ and $F = \Box(\Box \neg B \to \neg A)$. Then since C is equivalent to $\Box(B \to \Box \neg A)$, we easily get $(C \land E) \to \Box \neg B$; similarly we get $(D \land F) \to \Box \neg A$. (44) gives $E \lor F$, so Taut yields $(C \land D) \to (\Box \neg A \lor \Box \neg B)$, which, unpacking the definitions, is equivalent to (37).

Given (45), we get (35) and (38). For (45) and (34*) immediately yield (38), while (34*) and (45) by Sub yield $\Box A \to \Diamond \Box A$ and $\Diamond \Box A \to \Box \Diamond \Box A$, respectively, and (45*) and Becker yield $\Box \Diamond \Box A \to \Box \Box A$, and then (35) follows by Taut. We leave the proof of (45) as a theorem of **S5** to the reader.

3.5 REDUCTION OF MODALITIES

Parallel to the theory of reduction of tenses is a theory of reduction of modalities. In **T** already for any modalities $\triangle \triangledown$, or strings of boxes and diamonds, (34) and (34*) yield $\triangle \Box \triangledown A \to \triangle \triangledown A$ and $\triangle \triangledown A \to \triangle \Diamond \triangledown A$, using Sub to introduce $\triangledown$ and Becker to introduce $\triangle$. Thus we get an implication between any modality and the result of dropping a box anywhere or adding a diamond anywhere or (combining the two) weakening a box to a diamond anywhere. In particular if $\Box^m$ and $\Box^n$ denote strings of m and n boxes, respectively, we have $\Box^n A \to \Box^m A$ whenever $n > m$. To show these implications do not reverse, it will be enough to show for every m that there is a reflexive Kripke model $U = (U, \prec, V)$ and a state with $\Box^m p$ true at u while $\Box^{m+1} p$ is not. Indeed we may take U to consist of the natural numbers from 0 to $m + 1$, and let $u \prec v$ iff $v = u$ or $u + 1$, and let V make p true everywhere but at $m + 1$. Then $\Box^m p$ is true at 0 but $\Box^{m+1} p$ is not. Kripke models can be used to show that *no* implications between modalities hold except the "drop boxes and/or add diamonds" implications.

In **S4**, substitution in (35) gives $\Box\Box A \to \Box\Box\Box A$, which combined with the original (35) gives $\Box A \to \Box\Box\Box A$, and continuing in this way we get $\Box^n A \to \Box^m A$ for $n < m$ as well as for $m < n$, and $\Box^n A \leftrightarrow \Box^m A$ for any m and n. It follows that in any modality we may replace a string of boxes, or dually of diamonds, by another of a different length, thus expanding or contracting any string of modal operators of the same kind. The ultimate result is that every nonempty modality becomes equivalent to one of six kinds. (Counting in the empty modality $\varnothing$, with $\varnothing p$ being simply p, makes seven, and counting negations makes fourteen, the figure usually quoted in the literature as the number of modalities in **S4**.) The six are $\Box$, which (is equivalent to $\Box\Box\Box$ and so) implies $\Box\Diamond\Box$, which implies both of $\Diamond\Box$ and $\Box\Diamond$, each of which implies $\Diamond\Box\Diamond$, which implies ($\Diamond\Diamond\Diamond$ which is equivalent to) $\Diamond$. Showing that any other nonempty positive modality is equivalent to one of these six quickly reduces to showing that $\Diamond\Box\Diamond\Box$ is equivalent to $\Diamond\Box$ (and so, dually, $\Box\Diamond\Box\Diamond$ is equivalent to $\Box\Diamond$). And indeed $\Diamond\Box\Diamond\Box$ implies $\Diamond\Diamond\Diamond\Box$, equivalent to $\Diamond\Box$, which conversely is equivalent to $\Diamond\Box\Box\Box$ and so implies $\Diamond\Box\Diamond\Box$.

Kripke models can be used to show that none of the implications noted so far reverse: (i) even in **S4.3**, not even the conjunction of $\Box\Diamond\Box$ and $\varnothing$ implies $\Box$; (ii) even in **S4.3**, $\Box\Diamond\Box$ does not imply $\varnothing$; (iii) in **S4**, even the conjunction of $\Diamond\Box$ and $\Box\Diamond$ and $\varnothing$ does not imply $\Box\Diamond\Box$ (and dual nonimplications to (i)–(iii) equally hold).

Proofs. For claim (i), consider the Kripke model with states 0, 1, 2, with accessibility coinciding with $\leq$, the usual (nonstrict) order on natural numbers, and with p true at 0, false at 1, and true at 2. Then the model is not only reflexive and transitive but total, and $\Box\Diamond\Box p \wedge p$ is true at 0, but $\Box p$ is not. For claim (ii), the simpler model with states 0, 1, again with accessibility coinciding with $\leq$, and with p true at 1 only, suffices. For claim (iii), consider the reflexive, transitive Kripke model with the states consisting of all natural numbers and one additional state i; with accessibility coinciding with $\leq$ for the natural numbers, and with in addition i accessible from 0 and itself but from no other state; and with p true at all even natural numbers and at i. Then p is true at 0; also, $\Box\Diamond p$ is true at 0 because p and hence $\Diamond p$ is true at 0 and at i, and for any positive natural number m, p is true either at m or at $m + 1$, and $\Diamond p$ is true at m in either case; also, $\Diamond\Box p$ is true at 0 because $\Box p$ is true at i. But $\Box\Diamond\Box p$ is not true at 0 because $\Diamond\Box p$ is not true at 1, because at any positive natural number m, p is false either at m or at $m + 1$.

In **S4.2**, we have of course the additional implication (36), and this results in $\Box\Diamond\Box A$ becoming equivalent to $\Diamond\Box A$ (and dually $\Diamond\Box\Diamond A$ to $\Box\Diamond A$). For $\Diamond\Box A$ implies $\Diamond\Box\Box A$, which implies $\Box\Diamond\Box A$ by (36). So we are down to four nonempty modalities: $\Box$ implies $\Diamond\Box$, which implies $\Box\Diamond$, which implies $\Diamond$. We have already seen that even in **S4.3** we do not get any more implications. In **S5** $\Box$ and $\Diamond\Box$ become equivalent (and dually $\Box\Diamond$ and $\Diamond$), and we are left with $\Box$ and $\Diamond$ as the only modalities. This is a special case of a general theorem, to be treated a bit later, according to which every formula is provably equivalent in **S5** to a *flat* formula, one with no modalities inside modalities.

3.6 Completeness

Each of six modal logics has been proved to be sound for a certain class of frames. In fact, each of the six is also complete for that class of frames, though the proof takes more work. Consider **K** to begin with. Completeness says that validity implies demonstrability, which is equivalent to saying that indemonstrability implies invalidity; and since the invalidity of a formula is equivalent to the satisfiability of its negation, and the indemonstrability of a formula to the consistency of its negation, it is also equivalent to saying that consistency implies satisfiability. The proof of this implication, which involves a series of lemmas, is inevitably rather technical. The reader not wishing to tackle all the technicalities is urged to read at least the *statements* of the lemmas, to get an idea of the overall strategy and structure of the completeness proof, even if the *proofs* of the lemmas are skipped over.

So, given a consistent formula A we must show that it is satisfiable, which is to say, we must find a Kripke model and a state thereof where A is true. The key notion for the proof is that of a *maximal* consistent set, a set of formulas that is not itself inconsistent but becomes so if even one further formula is added to it. The first crucial fact about maximal consistent sets is the following, known as *Lindenbaum's lemma*:

(46) If t is a consistent set of formulas, then t is a subset of u for some maximal consistent set of formulas u.

Proof. The key is the observation that it is possible to enumerate all the formulas of the language in a list indexed by natural numbers: $A_0, A_1, A_2, \ldots$ For since there are only several dozen characters on the keyboard, we can assign each a two-digit code number in the range 10–99. Stringing together the digits for the code numbers of the characters in a formula having n of them, we obtain a $2n$-digit numeral denoting a code number $< 10^{2n}$ for the formula. We can then list all formulas in order of increasing code number. Then given a consistent set t we can form a sequence of larger and larger consistent sets $t = t_0 \subseteq t_1 \subseteq t_2 \subseteq \ldots$ by considering for each n whether adding A_n to t_n would result in inconsistency or not, and forming t_{n+1} by adding A_n to t_n if not, and leaving t_n unchanged if so. The union u of all the t_n will be consistent, since any finite subset will be a subset of some t_n, but adding any formula A_n not already in u to u will result in inconsistency, else A_n would already have been added at the nth stage of the construction.

Given Lindenbaum's lemma, the proof of completeness reduces to proving that for any maximal consistent set u there is a Kripke model with a state where every formula in u is true. Towards proving this result we have two more lemmas, establishing the properties of *deductive closure* and *bisectiveness* for maximal consistent sets.

(47)   If formula B is a consequence of maximal consistent set u, then B is an element of u.

Proof. If C is deducible from $B_1, \ldots, B_m$, and each B_j is deducible from $A_1, \ldots, A_n$, then C is deducible from the A_i. For

$$(A_1 \land \ldots \land A_n) \to C$$

is a tautological consequence of

$$(B_1 \land \ldots \land B_n) \to C$$
$$(A_1 \land \ldots \land A_n) \to B_1$$
$$\vdots$$
$$(A_1 \land \ldots \land A_n) \to B_m$$

And similarly, if a consistent set is enlarged by adding formulas that are deducible from it, no inconsistency results. It follows that a maximal consistent set, one incapable of enlargement without losing consistency, must already contain every formula deducible from it.

(48)   If $A \lor B$ is an element of maximal consistent set u, then either A or B is an element of u.

Proof. If A is not in u, then by maximality $u \cup \{A\}$ is inconsistent, meaning that there are some finitely many elements C_i of u such that the following formula is a theorem:

$$\neg(C_1 \land \ldots \land C_m \land A)$$

Similarly, if B is not in u, there are some finitely many elements D_j of u such that the following formula is a theorem:

$$\neg(D_1 \land \ldots \land D_n \land B)$$

But then the following would be a theorem, being a tautological consequence:

$$\neg(C_1 \wedge \ldots \wedge C_m \wedge D_1 \wedge \ldots \wedge D_n \wedge (A \vee B))$$

Since $A \vee B$ is in u, this is the negation of a conjunction of elements of u, meaning that u is inconsistent, contrary to hypothesis.

Next, an easy corollary of our work so far:

(49) Let u be a maximal consistent set, and A and B formulas. Then:
    (a) $\neg A$ is in u iff A is not in u
    (b) $A \wedge B$ is in u iff A is in u and B is in u

Here part (b) is immediate from deductive closure. The proof of part (a) (which is equivalent to the assertion that exactly one of A and $\neg A$ is in u) is left to the reader.

For maximal consistent sets u and v we write $u \lhd v$ iff A is in v whenever $\square A$ is in u. Some crucial properties of this relation are enunciated in the following lemmas, the proof of the first of which is left to the reader.

(50) If u and v are maximal consistent sets,
    then $u \lhd v$ iff $\Diamond A$ is in u whenever A is in v
(51) If u is a maximal consistent set and $\Diamond A$ is in u,
    then there is a maximal consistent set v such that
    $u \lhd v$ and A is in v

Proof. It is enough to show that the set t consisting of A and all B such that $\square B$ is in u is consistent. For then by Lindenbaum's lemma it will be contained in a maximal consistent set v, and the presence in v of all B such that $\square B$ is in u will mean that $u \lhd v$. Thus we must show that if $\Diamond A$ and the $\square B_i$ are in u, and C is the conjunction of A and the B_i, then $\neg C$ is not demonstrable. By Nec* it is enough to show that $\neg \Diamond C$ is not demonstrable, and by consistency for this it is enough to show that $\Diamond C$ *is* demonstrable. And it is, since $\Diamond C$ is deducible from $\Diamond A$ and the $\square B_i$ by (27).

Now let the *canonical Kripke model* $\mathbf{U} = (U, \prec, V)$ be defined as follows. U is the set of all maximal consistent sets, $\prec$ the relation $\lhd$, and V the valuation that makes p true at u iff p is in u. We

57

are ready at last for the main lemma, which completes the proof of completeness:

(52)   For any u in U and any formula A, $U \vDash A[u]$ iff A is in u

The proof is by induction on complexity.

Proof. The lemma holds for atomic A by definition of V and the atomic clause in the definition of truth in a Kripke model. Supposing the lemma holds for B, it holds for $A = \neg B$ because we have

$$
\begin{array}{ll}
U \vDash \neg B[u] & \text{iff} \\
\text{not } U \vDash B[u] & \text{iff} \\
\text{not } (B \text{ is in } u) & \text{iff} \\
\neg B \text{ is in } u &
\end{array}
$$

Here the first "iff" is by the negation clause in the definition of truth in a Kripke model, the second is the "induction hypothesis" that the lemma holds for B, and the third is (49a). The conjunction case is similar, but using (49b); it is left to the reader.

Supposing the lemma holds for B, it holds for $A = \Box B$ because we have

$$
\begin{array}{ll}
U \vDash \Box B[u] & \text{iff} \\
U \vDash B[v] \text{ for all } v \text{ with } u \lhd v & \text{iff} \\
B \text{ is in } v \text{ for all } v \text{ with } u \lhd v & \text{iff} \\
\Box B \text{ is in } u &
\end{array}
$$

For the third "iff," the only difficult one, the "if" direction is immediate from the definition of $\lhd$. For the "only if" direction, if $\Box B$ is *not* in u, then $\neg \Box B$ is in u by (49a), and its equivalent $\Diamond \neg B$ is in u by deductive closure, so there is a v with $u \lhd v$ and $\neg B$ in v by (51), and since B is not in v by (49a) again, the condition that B is in v for all v with $u \lhd v$ is not fulfilled.

This completes the proof of completeness for **K**. We can prove that **T** is complete for the class of reflexive models by showing that for **T** the relation $\lhd$ is reflexive. Similarly, we can prove that

S4 is complete for the class of reflexive and transitive models by showing that for **S4** the relation $\lhd$ is transitive. For **S4.2** what must be shown is that $\lhd$ is R-convergent. For **S4.3** what must be shown is that $\lhd$ is R-total. For **S5** what must be shown is that $\lhd$ is symmetric.

Proofs. For **T**, if u is a maximal consistent set and $\Box A$ is in u, then by axiom (34), A is deducible from u and so by deductive closure is in u, showing that $u \lhd u$ and $\lhd$ is reflexive. For **S4**, if u and v and w are maximal consistent sets and $u \lhd v$ and $v \lhd w$, and if $\Box A$ is in u, then by axiom (35), $\Box\Box A$ is deducible from u and so by deductive closure is in u, whence $\Box A$ is in v, whence A is in w, showing that $u \lhd w$ and $\lhd$ is transitive. For **S4.2**, if u and v and w are maximal consistent sets and $u \lhd v$ and $u \lhd w$, then we must show that there is a maximal consistent t with $v \lhd t$ and $w \lhd t$. For this it is enough to show that the set t_0 of all A such that $\Box A$ is in v together with all B such that $\Box B$ is in w is consistent, and then apply Lindenbaum's lemma. Well, if there were an inconsistency, it is easy to see using (26) that there would be a single $\Box A$ in v and a single $\Box B$ in w such that $\neg(A \wedge B)$, hence $\neg\Diamond(A \wedge B)$ is demonstrable. But this cannot be, because by (50) the presence of $\Box A$ in v means $\Diamond\Box A$ is in u, and the presence of $\Box B$ in w means $\Diamond\Box B$ is in u, and using (36), $\Box\Diamond B$ is in u. But from $\Diamond\Box A$ and $\Box\Diamond B$ are deducible $\Diamond(\Box A \wedge \Diamond B)$, and then $\Diamond\Diamond(A \wedge B)$, and then $\Diamond(A \wedge B)$, so this last formula is in u and cannot be inconsistent. For **S4.3**, if u and v and w are maximal consistent sets and $u \lhd v$ and $u \lhd w$, then we must show that either $v \lhd w$ or $w \lhd v$. Well, if not there is some A with $\Box A$ in v and A not in w and some B with $\Box B$ in w and B not in v. But this cannot be, since by (37) and bisectiveness, either $\Box(\Box A \to B)$ is in u, hence $\Box A \to B$ in v, or $\Box(\Box B \to A)$ is in u, hence $\Box B \to A$ in w. For **S5**, if u and v are maximal consistent sets and $u \lhd v$, we must show that $v \lhd u$. By (35) it is enough to show for any A in u that $\Diamond A$ is in v. Well, by (38) if A is in u then $\Box\Diamond A$ is in u and so given $u \lhd v$, $\Diamond A$ is in v.

3.7 DECIDABILITY

Let us return to **K**. Two refinements of the completeness theorem hold. The first refinement says that if A is consistent, then A is satisfiable in an *irreflexive* Kripke model, one where for *no u* do we have $u \prec u$. The existence of an irreflexive model may not seem especially interesting for **K**, but it is what we would want intuitively for temporal logic, and the proof to be given for **K** can be adapted to many temporal logics, though the details will be omitted here. There are two ways to get the desired irreflexive model. On the one hand, there is a technique (called "bulldozing") for transforming the canonical model into an irreflexive model. On the other hand, an irreflexive model can be obtained by replacing the "all at once" construction of the canonical model by a "step-by-step" construction.

Proof. The construction will be indicated only in outline. We start with the frame $(\Sigma, <_\Sigma)$ of finite sequences of positive integers with the immediate extension relation, which is irreflexive, as is any subframe $(S, <_\Sigma)$ consisting of a subset S of Σ with the same order relation (restricted to that subset). We will step-by-step attach to each s in Σ or some subset S thereof a maximal consistent set u_s. To begin with, we apply Lindenbaum's lemma and choose a maximal consistent set $u_\emptyset$ containing A, and attach it to $\emptyset$. Next we list all formulas in $u_\emptyset$ that begin with a diamond: $\Diamond B_1$, $\Diamond B_2$, $\Diamond B_3 \ldots$ For each i we apply (51) and choose a maximal consistent set u_i containing B_i and having $u_\emptyset \prec u_i$ and attach this u_i to i. Then for each i we repeat the process, and list all formulas in u_i that begin with a diamond: $\Diamond B_{i1}$, $\Diamond B_{i2}$, $\Diamond B_{i3} \ldots$ For each j we apply (51) and choose a maximal consistent set u_{ij} containing B_{ij} and having $u_i \prec u_{ij}$ and attach this u_{ij} to i, j. And so on. If it happens for some s that there are no formulas at all of form $\Diamond C$ in u_s then we leave u_t undefined for t properly extending s. In the end we have sets u_s assigned to all s in Σ or some subset S. We then consider the valuation V that for any sentence letter p and finite sequence s makes p true at s iff p is in u_s. The same proof as was used for the main lemma shows that in the Kripke model $(S, <_\Sigma, V)$ a formula B is true at s iff it belongs to u_s. So in particular, A is true at $u_\varnothing$, to complete the proof. (In doing a similar construction for $\mathbf{L}^\star$, we would start with $(\mathbb{Q}, <^\mathbb{Q})$.)

A second refinement says that if A is consistent, then A is satisfiable in some *finite* Kripke model, a result expressed by saying that $\mathbf{K}$ has the *finite model property*. There are two ways to get the desired finite model. On the one hand, there is a technique (called "filtration") for extracting a finite model from the canonical model. On the other hand, a finite model can be obtained by "miniaturizing" the construction of the canonical model.

> *Proof.* The construction will be indicated only in outline. We define an A-formula to be any formula that is either a subformula of A or the negation of a subformula of A. Instead of considering maximal consistent sets of formulas, we consider maximal consistent sets of A-formulas, which is to say, consistent sets of A-formulas that become inconsistent if even one more A-formula is added. Since there are only finitely many A-formulas, there are only finitely many maximal consistent sets of A-formulas. The construction of the canonical model can then be carried out using maximal consistent sets of A-formulas rather than maximal consistent sets, and results in a finite model for A, to complete the proof. Bells and whistles can be added to establish the finite model property for other modal and temporal logics as well.

The finite model property is of interest because in conjunction with completeness it implies decidability. First, note that if A contains only the first k sentence letters, we need only consider Kripke models that assign truth values only to those sentence letters. Second, recall from the discussion in section 1.8 that if we settle the truth value of a sentence in one model, we have settled its truth value in all isomorphic models. Since every Kripke model whose domain has n elements is isomorphic to a model where the domain is $\{1, 2, \ldots, n\}$, the effect of searching through all Kripke models of size n is achieved by searching through all

Kripke models with $U = \{1, 2, \ldots, n\}$, *and of these there are only finitely many.* (The reader can compute exactly how many, as a function of n and k.)

To be sure, the procedure of searching systematically through all Kripke models with $U = \{1\}$, then through all Kripke models with $U = \{1, 2\}$, and so on, not stopping until we find a model where $\neg A$ is satisfiable, is a mechanical procedure that will *not* by itself in all cases in a finite amount of time tell us whether a given formula A is valid or not. If the formula is invalid, then by the finite model property, this procedure will tell us so in a finite amount of time; but if the formula is valid, it will never stop or tell us anything. Similarly, the procedure of searching systematically through all proofs, not stopping until we find a proof of A, is a mechanical procedure that will *not* by itself in all cases in a finite amount of time tell us whether a given formula is valid or not. If the formula is valid, then by the completeness theorem this procedure will tell us so in a finite amount of time; but if the formula is invalid, it will never stop or tell us anything. However, if we combine the two one-sided procedures, doing a step of model searching, then a step of proof searching, back and forth, over and over, in a finite amount of time we will either find a model showing $\neg A$ satisfiable or a proof showing $\neg A$ unsatisfiable, and we will have a decision. The combination of completeness with the finite model property can be used to establish decidability for other modal and temporal logics.

For any Kripke model $\boldsymbol{U} = (U, \prec, V)$, write $u \prec^n v$ if there exist $n + 1$ states u_i such that $u = u_0 \prec u_1 \prec \ldots \prec u_n = v$ (so $\prec^1$ is just $\prec$ and $\prec^0$ is just $=$). A little thought shows that the truth value at u of a formula with modalities nested at most n deep depends only on the truth values of atomic formulas at v with $u \prec^m v$ for some $m \leq n$. Thus we could throw away all other v and the truth values of all formulas at u would be the same in the resulting smaller Kripke model $\boldsymbol{U}_u = (U_u, \prec_u, V_u)$, where U_u is the set of v such that $u \prec^m v$ for some m, and $\prec_u$ and V_u are simply the restrictions of $\prec$ and V to such v. This fact is sometimes dignified with the title of the *generated submodels theorem*.

In particular, for a classical formula (no modalities) we could throw away all v other than u, and for a flat formula (no modalities inside modalities) we could throw away all v other than u and the v with $u \prec v$. This last fact has an interesting consequence. If a flat formula A is true at any u in a Kripke model U based on any reflexive frame $(U, \prec)$, then A is true at some u in a Kripke model U' based on a reflexive, transitive, symmetric frame $(U', \prec')$. Indeed, one obtains U' by throwing away all v from U except u and the v with $u \prec v$, which by reflexivity includes u itself, and one obtains $\prec'$ by declaring all such surviving v accessible from each other. The valuation remains unchanged, and so the value of any classical formula at any v remains unchanged, and the value of any flat formula at u, which depends only on the values of classical formulas at v with $u \prec v$, remains unchanged as well. In particular, if A was true at u in U it remains true at u in U'. It follows that **T** and all the other systems considered above up to and including **S5** have the same flat formulas as theorems. For if A is flat and *not* a theorem of **T**, by completeness of **T** for reflexive models, $\neg A$ is true somewhere in a reflexive model, and so by what we have just shown $\neg A$ is true somewhere in a reflexive, transitive, symmetric model, and then by the soundness of **S5** for such models, A is not a theorem of **S5**.

For a reflexive and transitive Kripke model U, $\prec^n$ reduces to $\prec$, so U_u as defined above may be more simply described as the set U_u of v such that $u \prec v$, together with the restrictions of $\prec$ and V to such v, and the truth value of a formula at u in U will be the same as its truth value at u in U_u. If $\prec$ is also symmetric, it is easily seen that all states in U_u are accessible from each other (since $u \prec v$ and $u \prec w$ imply $v \prec u$ by symmetry and $v \prec w$ by transitivity). It follows that a formula A is valid for **S5** iff it is true at every state in every model of this special kind, so we can restrict our attention to models of this kind. But for models of this special kind, there is no need to mention $\prec$ at all. In place of (13) we can simply say

(53) $U \vDash \Box A[u]$ iff $U \vDash A[v]$ for all v

Also, the translation into predicate logic becomes a translation into *monadic* predicate logic, since we can simply set

(54) $(\Box A)^* = \forall x A^*$

63

A formula A will be demonstrable in **S5** iff its translation A^* is valid in *monadic* predicate logic, the part of classical predicate logic with only one-place predicates. But a great deal has been established in classical logic about monadic predicate logic, including not only the finite model property but also a *reduction to normal form*. According to this result, every monadic predicate formula having at most the one free variable x is equivalent to a disjunction whose disjuncts are conjunctions of formulas of the form C or $\forall x C$ or $\exists x C$, where C is a conjunction of atomic and negated atomic formulas $(\neg)P_i x$. This result immediately transfers to **S5** to give the flattening theorem mentioned earlier.

3.8 LOGICAL MODALITIES

Which of the many modal systems (if any) is the *right* one? In temporal logic, logicians limit themselves to laying out the options for physicists and others, first developing a minimal temporal logic with no special assumptions on the time order, and then showing how various assumptions on the time order correspond to various additional laws of temporal logic. In modal logic, logicians may still wish to pass on the question of which special assumptions are appropriate to physicists or metaphysicians or epistemologists or ethicists, if it is a question of physical or metaphysical or epistemic or deontic modalities. But there is no other discipline to which logic can pass off difficult questions about logical modality, alethic or apodictic. It is really incumbent upon logic, and not some other discipline, not just to lay out the options, but to make a choice among them.

The principles of the minimal modal logic seem intuitively correct for just about *any* notion of necessity. This includes the apodictic "it is demonstrable by pure logic that" and the alethic "it is true by virtue of logical form alone that." Likewise the axiom (34). If it is demonstrable by pure logic that A or true by virtue of logical form alone that A, then it is true that A. Likewise the axiom (35). If we have demonstrated that A, then simply by exhibiting that demonstration we can demonstrate that it is demonstrable that A. And if it is a fact that A is true by virtue of logical form alone, and anything else of the same logical form as A would equally be true, then the fact that A is true by virtue of logical form also would be equally true of anything else of the same logical form as A, and is true by virtue of logical form alone. So we would seem to get *at least* the system **S4** for both apodictic and alethic logical modality.

What about the distinguishing axiom $A \to \Box \Diamond A$ of **S5**? If it is true that A, then it is clearly not demonstrably *un*true that A, and not by virtue of logical form *un*true that A, so we have $\neg \Box \neg A$ or $\Diamond A$, for either sense of the box $\Box$. But the "demonstration" just given was not a categorical demonstration by pure logic alone but only a hypothetical demonstration based on a certain assumption, namely, the assumption that A. So we cannot, at least not on the strength of the considerations brought forward so far, conclude that $\Box \Diamond A$ in the apodictic case. By contrast, in the alethic case, if it is a fact that A is not untrue by virtue of logical form alone, then that fact itself is true by virtue of logical form alone, so we *can* conclude that $\Box \Diamond A$ in the alethic case, so we would seem to get *at least* the system **S5** for alethic modality.

In fact, to the extent that there is any conventional wisdom about the question, it is that **S5** is correct for alethic logical modality, and **S4** correct for apodictic logical modality. However, nothing said so far constitutes even an informal "proof" that no formula not a theorem of **S4** is correct for apodictic logical modality, or that no formula not a theorem of **S5** is correct for alethic modality. And indeed there is no generally accepted informal argument for the first claim, though a convincing one can be given for the second claim.

What is to be shown is that if a formula A is not a theorem of **S5**, then it has an instance that intuitively is not true if the box is read as "it is true by virtue of logical form that." What we know is that if A is not a theorem of **S5**, then there is a finite Kripke model of a special kind, consisting simply of a set U *all* of whose states count as accessible from each other and a function V assigning to each u in U and each sentence letter p a truth value, and a u in U where A is not true. What we must show is that from such a model we can produce an instance of A that intuitively is not true.

Chapter Three

The process of doing so may be illustrated by the following example A:

(55) $\quad \Box((p \wedge q) \vee (q \wedge r) \vee (r \wedge p)) \to (\Box p \vee \Box q \vee \Box r)$

(55) is not a theorem of **S5**, and there is a Kripke model with three states x, y, z with p true at x and y, q true at y and z, and r true at z and x, where (55) is untrue at some (indeed, as it happens, every) state.

To get an instance where (55) is intuitively untrue, we assume we have at least two sentences that have no pertinent logical structure and are logically independent of each other, say, $H_1 = $ "This coin will come up heads on the first toss" and $H_2 = $ "This coin will come up heads on the second toss." Out of these we may form the four basic conjunctions $H_1 \wedge H_2$ and $H_1 \wedge \neg H_2$ and $\neg H_1 \wedge H_2$ and $\neg H_1 \wedge \neg H_2$, and logical form alone guarantees that exactly one of them will be true. What we will want is *three* combinations with this property, one for each of the states in the model, so let us take the first two of the four basic conjunctions, $H_1 \wedge H_2$ and $H_1 \wedge \neg H_2$, and as a third the disjunction of the remaining two, or what is equivalent, $\neg H_1$. Let us call these three X and Y and Z. Now let us substitute for p, which in the model is true at x and y, the disjunction P of X and Y, and for q, true at y and z, the disjunction Q of Y and Z, and for r, true at z and x, the disjunction R of Z and X. P amounts to "This coin will come up heads on the first toss," Q to "If the coin comes up heads on the first toss, it will come up tails on the second toss," R to "If the coin comes up heads on the first toss, it will come up heads on the second toss." Then three and only three combinations of truth values for P and Q and R are logically possible, namely, those represented by the values of p and q and r at x and at y and at z in the model. By virtue of logical form alone, we may have P true and Q false and R true, or P true and Q true and R false, or P false and Q true and R true, and no other combination. And just as A comes out false in the model, the instance of A that results on substituting P and Q and R for p and q and r comes out intuitively false.

Something similar can be done for *any* formula that fails in a model for **S5**, but the proof of the general result, *Carnap's theorem*, is beyond the scope of the present work.

3.9 QUANTIFICATION

The results of the experiment of combining classical predicate logic with modal sentential logic are even more curious and even less satisfactory than for temporal logic. The derivations of the temporal converse Barcan formula and the permanence of identity become derivations of a modal converse Barcan formula and the necessity of identity if we simply change future into modal operators. For the direct Barcan formula and the permanence of nonidentity we would have to change past operators into modal operators as well, but then the temporal axiom $A \rightarrow$ **GP**A translates into $A \rightarrow$ $\Box\Diamond A$, which is *not* an axiom of the minimal modal logic, and indeed of the six systems we have been studying is available only in **S5**. For weaker systems we still get one counterintuitive formula (converse Barcan) though we no longer get another (direct Barcan), and we still get one intuitive formula (necessity of identity) though we no longer get another (necessity of nonidentity).

If metaphysical modality is at issue, in philosophical respects the situation will be much the same as when temporality was at issue. A metaphysical doctrine of contingently concrete entities will correspond to the metaphysical doctrine of temporarily concrete entities. The *potentialist* as opposed to *actualist* "there could have been" quantifier will correspond to the eventualist as opposed to presentist "there have been or are or are going to be" quantifier. A distinction between "she would have been as rich as he would have been" and "she would have been as rich as he is" will correspond to the distinction between "she will be as rich as he will be" and "she will be as rich as he is." The reader will find it instructive to try to work out the analogy. (One disanalogy is that far more philosophers have been willing to junk the grammatical category of tense and attribute tenseless being equally to all things there have been or are or are going to be, than have been willing to junk the grammatical category of mood and attribute moodless being equally to all things there are or could have been. Whether this is more than just a prejudice is a question the logician *qua* logician need not address.)

For various other kinds of modality, there is a further—or rather, the prior—problem that the very idea of combining quantification with them makes questionable sense. Historically, the problem, *Quine's critique*, was raised originally for the conception of necessity as analyticity. The problem is over what is called *de re* as contrasted with *de dicto* modality, as exemplified by $\exists x\Box Px$ as contrasted with $\Box\exists xPx$. What can be meant by

(56) "it is analytic that Px" is satisfied by a

given that analyticity is a notion that in the first instance applies to complete sentences?

If we try to define (56) to hold iff for some expression t denoting a we have

(57) "it is analytic that Pt" is true

we face the problem that (57) may hold for some choices of t and not for others, and there seems no way to select for each thing a one *canonical* denoting expression for it. In the stock example, Px is "$x =$ the brightest star of the evening." Put in "the brightest star of the evening" for x and you get something presumably analytic, put in "the brightest star of the morning" for x and you get something presumably synthetic. The problem remains if definite descriptions are replaced by proper names, as when Px is taken to be "$x =$ Hesperus." Put in "Hesperus" for x and you get something analytic, "Hesperus = Hesperus"; put in "Phosphorus" for x and you get something synthetic, "Phosphorus = Hesperus." And it would be completely arbitrary to declare "Hesperus" canonical and "Phosphorus" apocryphal, and proclaim that the planet which goes by both these names satisfies "it is analytic that $x =$ Hesperus" but not "it is analytic that $x =$ Phosphorus." Indeed, the only plausible example of a nonarbitrary choice of canonical denoting expressions in the literature is the choice of numerals as canonical denoting expressions for natural numbers. (There are different systems of numerals, of course, but something like "1999 = MCMXCIX," unlike something like "Hesperus = Phosphorus," is plausibly regarded as analytic.)

Whether the objection extends to logical necessity (in either sense, as validity or as demonstrability), to the necessary as the *a priori*, or to epistemic necessity, is controversial (since even those who agree that it is not analytic that Hesperus = Phosphorus may disagree over whether it is necessary in one or another of these other senses). The most common view today is that the objection does *not* extend to metaphysical necessity. (On the most common view, identities between proper names are *metaphysically* necessary, just as they are permanent, and "it is metaphysically necessary that Px" is satisfied by a thing iff "it is metaphysically necessary that Pt" is true for some, or equivalently any, proper name t for that thing, just as "it is permanently the case that Px" is satisfied by a thing iff "it is permanently the case that Pt" is true for some, or equivalently any, proper name t for that thing. Underlying this view is an intuition of rigidity for metaphysical modal contexts parallel to the intuition of rigidity for temporal contexts; how far this intuition extends to other kinds of modality is controversial, though the common view is that it anyhow does not extend to analyticity.) These topics depend so heavily on philosophy of language, however, that they cannot be further pursued here.

Suffice it to say that what was said about temporal predicate logic goes double for modal predicate logic: there remains a good deal of work to be done before it can be said to be in a satisfactory state. The main philosophical lesson that one can draw from work on formal systems of quantified modal logic is that one should be very wary of drawing philosophical lessons from work on formal systems of quantified modal logic.

3.10 FURTHER READING

The handbook chapter Bull & Segerberg (1984) treats a vast array of systems, and has good coverage of the older algebraic model theory, omitted in the present chapter. (The authors are among the highest authorities in the field. R. A. Bull, among many other contributions, was a pioneer of *hybrid logic*, a cross between the regimented and autonomous approaches. Krister Segerberg was a pioneer in the development of such techniques as bulldozing and filtration.) The historical sections of this chapter, however, having stimulated further work, have by now been superseded by the definitive study Goldblatt (2006). Among other original sources, Lewis & Langford (1932) and Kripke (1963) are still widely read; see Carnap (1946) for, among other things, "Carnap's theorem." Harrel (1984) surveys early work in *dynamic logic*, a pioneering application of modal logic to computer science—a project which has since grown to immense size. An excellent and up-to-date book-length treatment, though more directed to students of mathematics or computer science than of philosophy, is Blackburn, de Rijke, & Venema (2002). For *provability logic*, a subfield not covered here, the most comprehensive reference is Boolos (1993). The issue of which modal logic is the right one for logical modalities is addressed in Burgess (1999) and a sequel, Burgess (2003). Garson (1984) is a notable attempt to bring order to the scene of chaos that is quantified modal logic. A definitive treatment of the comparative expressive power of the regimented and autonomous approaches (with *actuality operators* and related devices) is provided by Cresswell (1990). See Quine (1953) and Burgess (1998) and Neale (2000) for the original version of "Quine's critique," a later defense of it, and a definitive treatment of its history. For the linguistics of mood and modality (dynamic, epistemic, and deontic), taking account of a wide variety of world languages, see Palmer (1986).

Conditional Logic

4.1 INDICATIVE AND COUNTERFACTUAL CONDITIONALS

Conditionals are instances of "if A, B" or "B, if A." The A-position is called the *antecedent* or *protasis* position and the B-position the *consequent* or *apodasis* position. Conditionals come in two types, generally distinguishable in English by the absence or presence of "would" in the consequent, the stock example of the contrast between them being the following pair:

(1) If Oswald did not shoot Kennedy, someone else did.
(2) If Oswald had not shot Kennedy, someone else would have.

The difference is easy to appreciate intuitively—almost anyone would agree to (1), but only a conspiracy theorist to (2)—though that does not mean it is easy to characterize theoretically.

There are two competing terminologies. On one terminology, type I is called "indicative" and type II "subjunctive," on the grounds that the former type is grammatically in the indicative or realis mood in most languages, and the latter type in the subjunctive or irrealis mood in many—though not so in many others. On the other terminology, type I is called factual and type II counterfactual, on the grounds that the former type does not while the latter does as a general rule suggest that the speaker believes that the antecedent is or may be contrary to fact—though "If it were a case of smallpox we'd see just these symptoms" may equally well follow "I don't accept your diagnosis of smallpox, but I'll have to admit that" or "You don't accept my diagnosis of smallpox, but you'll have to admit that." Here a mixed terminology will be used, and types I and II henceforth called indicative and counterfactual. For the space of this chapter the indicative and counterfactual conditionals will be symbolized $A \to B$ and

$A \Rightarrow B$, while $A \supset B$ and $A \sqsupset B$, called the *material* and *strict* conditionals, will be stipulatively defined to be abbreviations for $\neg A \lor B$ and $\Box(\neg A \lor B)$.

There are few if any occurrences of conditionals in the antecedents of conditionals (a fact for which a truly satisfactory theory of conditionals should be able to give an explanation), and few if any occurrences of "if A, then if B, then C" not equivalent to "if A and B, then C" (and to an intermediate form without symbolic counterpart, "if A, and if B, then C"). For this reason, until further notice we will consider only two types of formulas, *truth-functional* formulas, involving only $\neg$, $\land$, $\lor$, and *conditional* formulas of the form $A \rightarrow B$ or $A \Rightarrow B$ with A and B truth-functional.

Cutting across the indicative/counterfactual distinction is another illustrated by the following pairs:

(3) If Bill comes, then the party will be a great success.
(4) Even if Bill comes, still the party will be a great success.
(5) If Bill had come, then the party would have been a great success.
(6) Even if Bill had come, still the party would have been a great success.

Again the distinction is easy to appreciate intuitively—in (3) and (5) it is being suggested that Bill's coming is sufficiently conducive to the party's success, while in (4) and (6) what is being suggested is that Bill's coming is *in*sufficiently *in*conducive to success—but not so easy to characterize theoretically. There is no established terminology, but the rarer kind exemplified by (4) and (6) are sometimes called "noninterference" conditionals.

Classical logic treats the indicative conditional as a material conditional. The success of classical logic in application to mathematics strongly suggests that $\rightarrow$ as used in mathematics is true under the same conditions as $\supset$. Recognition of this fact still allows for a difference in a dimension of meaning that does not affect truth values, and leaves open the question of the relationship of $\rightarrow$ as used outside mathematics with $\supset$. It would be a point against a theory of the conditional if it had to be supposed that $\rightarrow$ means in mathematics something totally unrelated to what it means elsewhere, but it might well be that the meaning of $\rightarrow$ is something complex that reduces to something simpler in mathematical contexts owing to some special feature of mathematics (perhaps the fact that mathematics deals in certainties and not probabilities).

There is no classical theory of counterfactual conditionals to consider. Classical logic neglects them for the same reason it neglects temporal and modal distinctions, namely, that they play no serious role in mathematics. There is, however, to be considered the *modal* theory, or theory that identifies counterfactuals with strict conditionals. Since counterfactual conditionals are about what could potentially have been the case (not about what we don't know isn't actually the case), and since it seems we can contemplate counterfactually violations of the laws of nature, the modality involved presumably belongs to the metaphysical (rather than physical) species of the dynamic (rather than epistemic) genus. So long as we are excluding conditionals embedded inside conditionals, we get the same logic for strict conditionals for any of the systems **T** through **S5**, since as shown in section 3.7 they have the same flat formulas (formulas without modalities inside modalities) as theorems. Thus we may speak of "the" modal theory of counterfactual conditionals. But until further notice we restrict our attention to indicatives.

4.2 CONVERSATIONAL IMPLICATURE

Early critics of the classical theory gave examples where according to the theory a conditional should be true, because the antecedent clearly is (or has explicitly been assumed to be) false and/or the consequent true, but where the conditional would be something inappropriate to assert. To give a typical example:

(7)   The team will not lose every game this season.

(8)   The team will be invited to the postseason play-offs.

(9)   Therefore, if the team loses every game this season, it will be invited to the postseason play-offs.

The cogency of such examples was called into question by the *Gricean theory of conversational implicature*. Here *B* is called a conversational implicature of A if from the fact that A is asserted plus the assumption that the speaker is trying to be helpful the hearer can infer that B, where being helpful means trying to communicate as briefly as possible facts that are as informative, as reliable, and as pertinent as possible. For example, it is in general a conversational implicature of a disjunction that the speaker is not in a position to assert one of the disjuncts, since to assert a disjunct would be doubly more helpful—both briefer and more informative—than asserting the disjunction.

It had always been recognized that there are truths that it is not appropriate to assert for reasons of etiquette and so forth, but conversational implicature adds a whole new class of reasons why assertions may be inappropriate. It would be inappropriate to assert a disjunction when one was in a position to assert one of the disjuncts, since this would convey a false conversational implicature. Thus *even if* the conditional $A \rightarrow B$ meant nothing more than the disjunction $\neg A \vee B$, still it would be inappropriate to assert a conditional like (9) when one was in a position to assert its consequent (8) or the negation of its antecedent (7). Such considerations tend to neutralize the early objections to the classical theory.

Subsequent debate has concerned the conditions for the assert*i*bility of conditionals, defined as assert*a*bility apart from conversational implicatures (and reasons of etiquette and so forth). Later critics of the classical theory of indicative conditionals have given examples where a conditional intuitively can be asserted, though if $\rightarrow$ meant $\supset$, application of Gricean theory in a simple, straightforward way would suggest that it cannot be, because the consequent or the negation of the antecedent is asserted:

(10) It won't rain. If it does, we'll hold the party indoors.
(11) The party will be a success. Even if it rains, the party will be a success.

Counterexamples in philosophy are seldom if ever absolutely decisive, and a classical theorist might attempt to argue that a more subtle, sophisticated application of Gricean theory would allow such conditionals to be asserted. What resulted in a serious loss of supporters for the classical theory was not so much the accumulation of such anomalies as the development by critics of a rival theory with a definite criterion for the assertibility of conditionals.

4.3 THE PROBABILISTIC THEORY OF INDICATIVE CONDITIONALS

The rival theory involves the notion of probability. If we are considering truth-functional formulas involving the first k sentence letters, then there are 2^k possible models or valuations. For present purposes, a *probability function* π may be defined as simply an assignment of a nonnegative number c_V to each such valuation V, with the property that the sum of the c_V is one. The *probability* $\pi(A)$ of a formula is then the sum of the c_V for V that make A true, and the *uncertainty* $1 - \pi(A)$ of A the sum of the c_V for V that make A false.

Various elementary laws of the probability calculus found in the first pages of primers on the subject, such as the law $\pi(A \vee B) = \pi(A) + \pi(B) - \pi(A \wedge B)$, follow easily from this definition. Notably, tautologies have probability one, countertautologies have probability zero, and tautologically equivalent formulas have the same probability.

Generalizing this last, let us call an argument with truth-functional premises and conclusion *probabilistically valid* iff for every probability function the uncertainty of its conclusion is no more than the sum of the uncertainties of its premises, and *probabilistically countervalid* iff the sum of the uncertainties of the premises can be made as low as desired and the uncertainty of the conclusion as high as desired by suitable choice of probability function. Then probabilistic validity and countervalidity coincide with logical validity and invalidity.

Proof. Consider the argument from $A_1, \ldots, A_k$ to B. For any probability function, the uncertainty of B is the sum of the c_V for each V that makes B false, while the sum of the uncertainties of the A_i is the sum over all i of the sum of the c_V for each V that makes A_i false. If the argument is valid, every V that makes B false makes at least one of the A_i false, so every c_V appearing in the former sum appears at least once in the latter sum. But if the argument is invalid, there is a W that makes all the A_i true and B false, and for the probability function that sets $c_V = 1$ for $V = W$ and $c_V = 0$ for $V \neq W$, the sum of the uncertainties of the premises is zero and the uncertainty of the conclusion one.

The probability of B *conditional on* A is given by $\pi(B \mid A) = \pi(A \wedge B)/\pi(A)$. In general it is *not* equal to the probability of the material conditional, given by $\pi(A \supset B) = 1 - \pi(A \wedge \neg B)$. If we write a and b and c for the probabilities of $A \wedge B$ and $A \wedge \neg B$ and $\neg A$, then $\pi(B \mid A) = a/(a + b)$ while $\pi(p \supset q) = 1 - b = a + c$. We always have $\pi(B \mid A) \leq \pi(A \supset B)$, so whenever $\pi(B \mid A)$ is high, $\pi(A \supset B)$ will be high, but the converse fails, since $\pi(B \mid A)$ can be very close or even equal to zero when $\pi(A \supset B)$ is very close to one.

Proofs. For the positive point, $a + b \leq 1$, so $ab + b^2 \leq b$, so $0 \leq b - ab - b^2$, so $a \leq a + b - ab - b^2 = (a + b)(1 - b)$, so $a/(a + b) \leq 1 - b$. For the negative point, take $a = .00$, $b = .01$, $c = .99$.

In the "degenerate" case where A is *certainly* false, so that $\pi(A) = 0$, the formula $\pi(B \mid A) = \pi(A \wedge B)/\pi(A)$ gives $\pi(B \mid A) = 0/0$, which is undefined. $\pi(B \mid A)$ may be defined in this case by a special convention, but just as any convention as to the value of 0^0 will create an exception to one or the other of two laws, $x^0 = 1$ and $0^y = 0$, so any convention as to the value of $\pi(B \mid A)$ when $\pi(A) = 0$ will lead to a violation either of $\pi(A \mid A \wedge \neg B) = 1$ or of $\pi(A \mid B \wedge \neg A) = 0$. The convention that sets $\pi(B \mid A) = 1$ when $\pi(A) = 0$ is the most common and convenient.

We all assert things of which we are less than certain, but it is generally recognized that one ought to assert that A only if one's degree of belief that A is high. Sometimes it is said that one ought to assert that A only if one's subjective probability $\pi(A)$ that A is high. Strictly speaking such "probability" language is only appropriate if one is idealizing to the extent of assuming that degrees of belief have exact numerical values, and that these exact numerical values strictly obey the laws of the probability calculus. Since idealization is sometimes useful, let us fall in with this one for a while, without forgetting that it *is* an idealization.

Three proposed probabilistic criteria of assertibility have figured in debates over indicative conditionals:

(12) A is assertible iff $\pi(A)$ is high

(13) $A \to B$ is assertible iff $\pi(A \supset B)$ is high

(14) $A \to B$ is assertible iff $\pi(A \mid B)$ is high

Here (12) is widely—though not *universally*, since this is *philosophy*, after all—accepted, (13) is what (12) implies assuming the classical theory of indicative conditionals, and (14) is the rival criterion to (13) put forward by critics, known as the *Adams criterion*. Proponents of (14) as against (13) point to examples like (10) and (11), which their theory can neatly explain. If we are told that $\pi(\neg A)$ and/or that $\pi(B)$ is high there would be no point in telling us that $\pi(A \supset B)$ is high, since that follows immediately. But there would still be a point to telling us that $\pi(A \mid B)$ is high if it is, because $\pi(A \mid B)$ can be low even when $\pi(\neg A \land B)$ is high.

The Adams criterion is now widely accepted, but if there is widespread agreement that it holds, there is no generally accepted explanation why. The simplest hypothesis would be that (14) is just a special case of the ordinary criterion (12). This would be so if the conditional were a compound whose probability was equal to the conditional probability of its consequent given its antecedent. But according to the *Lewis trivialization theorem* there *is* no compound $A \, \S \, B$ for which we always have

(15) $\pi(A \, \S \, B) = \pi(B \mid A)$

At least, this is so given the background assumptions (which later versions of the result have somewhat relaxed) that $\S$ resembles $\to$ in two respects, namely, that $A \, \S \, (B \, \S \, C)$ is always equivalent to $(A \land B) \, \S \, C$, so that the two always have the same probability, and that $A \, \S \, B$ is not always equivalent to B, and the two sometimes have different probabilities.

> *Proof.* We show how (15) and the first background assumption lead to the negation of the second background assumption.

77

i $\pi(A \,\S\, (B \,\S\, C)) = \pi((A \wedge B) \,\S\, C)$

ii $\pi((B \,\S\, C) \mid A) = \pi(C \mid (A \wedge B))$

iii $\pi(B) = \pi(B \mid A) \cdot \pi(A) + \pi(B \mid \neg A) \cdot \pi(\neg A)$

iv $\pi(B \,\S\, A) = \pi(B \,\S\, A \mid B) \cdot \pi(A) + \pi(B \,\S\, A \mid \neg A) \cdot \pi(\neg A)$

v $\pi(B \,\S\, A) = \pi(A \mid A \wedge B) \cdot \pi(A) + \pi(A \mid \neg A \wedge B) \cdot \pi(\neg A)$

vi $\pi(A \mid B) = \pi(A \mid A \wedge B) \cdot \pi(A) + \pi(A \mid \neg A \wedge A) \cdot \pi(\neg A)$

vii $\pi(A \mid A \wedge B) = 1$

viii $\pi(A \mid \neg A \wedge B) = 0$

ix $\pi(A \mid B) = \pi(A)$

Here (i) is the first of our two background assumptions, (ii) follows from (15) and (i), (iii) is an elementary law of probability, (iv) is an instance of (iii), (v) follows from (ii) and (iv), (vi) follows from (15) and (v), (vii) and (viii) are elementary laws of probability, and (ix) follows from (vi)–(vii), and contradicts the second of our two background assumptions.

So it seems the indicative conditional is *not* a compound the probability of whose truth is equal to the conditional probability of its consequent given its antecedent, and (14) can*not* be explained as simply a special case of (12). In the wake of this result three main theories have emerged about the conditions under which indicative conditionals are true.

Materialism maintains that the indicative conditional is true under exactly the same conditions under which the material conditional is true, so that if the two conditionals are not strictly synonymous, the difference pertains only to some dimension of meaning perhaps affecting assertibility but not affecting truth values.

Idealism maintains that the indicative conditional is true just in case the conditional probability of its consequent given its antecedent is high, identifying the truth value as the "Assertibility value." Since we are speaking here of subjective probability, which varies from person to person, the conditions for the truth of an indicative conditional would also be subjective, and such a conditional might be true for one person and false for another.

Nihilism maintains that indicative conditionals simply do not have truth values but merely assertibility conditions (14) that are parallel to (rather than literally instances of) the assertibility conditions (12). A variant of nihilism is *semi*-nihilism, according to which an indicative conditional has the same truth value as its consequent if its antecedent is true, and no truth value if its antecedent is false. (This view is supported by appeal to an analogy between conditional assertions and conditional bets, conditional promises, conditional commands.) Another variant of nihilism is the *error* theory, according to which we use the indicative conditional *as if* it were a compound of the kind the Lewis trivialization theorem shows cannot exist.

Classical logic identifies being logically valid with preserving truth, leading from true premises to true conclusions, by virtue of form. If the probability that determines assertibility diverges from the probability of truth, however, there is room alongside the logic of truth-preservation for a logic of assertibility-preservation. With conditionals the latter logic will be the *only* logic that can be recognized by the nihilist, who recognizes no truth values for conditionals, and the idealist, who identifies the truth- and assertibility-conditions of conditionals.

An argument from conditional premises $A_i \rightarrow B_i$ to a conditional conclusion $C \rightarrow D$ will be called *probabilistically valid*, and the premises said to *probabilistically imply* or have as a *probabilistic consequence* the conclusion, iff for every probability function π, the conditional uncertainty $1 - \pi(D \mid C)$ of the conclusion is no greater than the sum of the conditional uncertainties $1 - \pi(B_i \mid A_i)$ of the premises, and *probabilistically countervalid* iff for every positive number ε however small there is some probability function π that makes each premise's conditional probability $\pi(B_i \mid A_i)$ at least $1 - \varepsilon$, but the conclusion's conditional probability $\pi(D \mid C)$ at most ε.

Among argument forms that are logically valid in the ordinary truth-preservation sense when the conditionals are read as material, there are some that are not probabilistically valid (and indeed are probabilistically countervalid), among them *hypothetical syllogism, a fortiori, contraposition*:

(16) from $A \rightarrow B$ and $B \rightarrow C$ to $A \rightarrow C$
(17) from $A \rightarrow C$ to $(A \wedge B) \rightarrow C$
(18) from $A \rightarrow \neg B$ to $B \rightarrow \neg A$

Counterexamples. Let ε be very small but positive. For (16), let the basic conjunctions $p \wedge q \wedge \neg r$ and $\neg p \wedge q \wedge r$ have the probabilities ε and $1 - ε$ and all other basic conjunctions probability 0. Then $\pi(p \wedge q)/\pi(p) = ε/ε = 1$, while $\pi(q \wedge r)/\pi(q) = (1 - ε)/1 = 1 - ε$, and $\pi(p \wedge r)/\pi(p) = 0/ε = 0$. For (17), let the basic conjunctions $p \wedge q \wedge \neg r$ and $p \wedge \neg q \wedge r$ have probabilities ε and $1 - ε$ and all other basic conjunctions probability 0. Then $\pi(p \wedge r)/\pi(p) = (1 - ε)/1 = 1 - ε$, while $\pi(p \wedge q \wedge r)/\pi(p \wedge q) = 0/ε = 0$. For (18), let the basic conjunctions and $p \wedge q$ and $p \wedge \neg q$ have probabilities ε and $1 - ε$, and the other basic conjunctions probability 0. Then $\pi(p \wedge \neg q)/\pi(p) = (1 - ε)/1 = 1 - ε$, while $\pi(q \wedge \neg p)/\pi(q) = 0/ε = 0$.

Ordinary-language instances of hypothetical syllogism and *a fortiori* and contraposition can now be given where the premises have high conditional probability and so are assertible by the Adams criterion, but the conclusion has low conditional probability and so is unassertible by the Adams criterion—and where, it is claimed, the premises are intuitively assertible and the conclusion intuitively unassertible. It is traditional to use examples pertaining to elections.

At the time of this writing, the campaign for the 2008 U. S. presidential election is still in its early stages, and the party primary elections to choose candidates for the general election have not yet taken place. Future-tense examples pertaining to one party's primary and to the subsequent general election will be used. The reader should be willing to assume for the sake of the examples that Clinton and Obama are overwhelmingly likely to come in either first and second or second and first in the Democratic primary, and that they could both be on the general election ballot only if there were a split in their party, making a loss certain.

(19)   If Clinton wins the primary, Obama will come in second.
       If Obama dies before the primary, Clinton will win it.
       So, if Obama dies before the primary, he will come in second.

(20) If Obama is on the general election ballot, the
      Democrats will win.
      So, if Clinton and Obama are both on the general
      election ballot, the Democrats will win.
(21) If Clinton wins, she won't win by a landslide.
      So, if Clinton wins by a landslide, she won't win.

Similar examples in the past rather than the future tense are also
possible. (Imagine people who have gone off into the wilderness
about the time of this writing, and have remained out of contact
with civilization for a year or so, speculating around the campfire
about the results of elections that have taken place in their absence; then consider the past-tense versions of (19)–(21).)

4.4 THE REMOTENESS THEORY OF INDICATIVE CONDITIONALS

If we try to state as much as we can of (12)–(14) in qualitative
rather than quantitative terms, dropping the idealization involved
in probability talk for something perhaps more realistic, we would
have to say something like this:

(22) A is assertible iff one's degree of belief that A is high
(23) $A \rightarrow B$ is assertible iff one's degree of belief that $A \supset B$
      is high
(24) $A \rightarrow B$ is assertible iff one's degree of belief that $A \wedge B$
      is high (at least) compared to one's degree of belief that
      A (which may be low)

or equivalently, this:

(25) A is assertible iff one's degree of belief that $\neg A$ is low
(26) $A \rightarrow B$ is assertible iff one's degree of belief that $A \wedge \neg B$
      is low
(27) $A \rightarrow B$ is assertible iff one's degree of belief that $A \wedge \neg B$
      is low (even) compared to one's degree of belief that A
      (which may already be low)

Here "one's degree of belief that C is low" means something
like "low enough that the (epistemic) possibility that C can be   81

safely neglected." (The qualifier "probably" should be added if the relevant degree of belief is lowish but not quite so low as to be negligible.) But how low is low enough for (unqualified) assertion? The answer surely must vary from situation to situation, with a higher cutoff for and hence a looser standard of assertion for casual table talk than for court testimony, for instance.

One route towards a more realistic qualitative alternative to the highly idealized quantitative probabilistic approach begins with the colloquial qualitative and comparative expressions "remote possibility" and "more remote possibility," both quite common in English. (They drew 600,000 and 12,000 Google hits, respectively, when the author tried them.) In such language the competing materialist and Adams criteria (26) and (27) might be reformulable as follows:

(28) $A \to B$ is assertible iff $A \wedge \neg B$ is a remote possibility (enough so that it can safely be neglected)

(29) $A \to B$ is assertible iff $A \wedge \neg B$ is a remote possibility (even) compared to the possibility that A (which may already be remote)

("Remote from *what*?" The answer cannot be "reality," because *all* epistemic possibilities are candidates for how things may so far as we know really be. The answer would seem rather to be "credibility.") This heuristic idea can be given a more technical treatment.

So let us consider models of the kind $U = (U, \leq, V)$, thought of intuitively in the following way. The elements of U represent epistemically possible states of the world, ways that for all we know the world may actually be. The relation $u \leq v$ is thought of (*not* as a mysterious relative-possibility relation but) as an intuitive nonstrict relative-remoteness relation, "u is a no more remote possibility than v," in terms of which we can define a strict relative-remoteness relation, "u is a less remote possibility than v" by taking $u < v$ to hold if $u \leq v$ holds and $v \leq u$ fails. The valuation V is thought of in the by-now familiar way as telling us which p are true at which u.

A truth-functional formula A will have truth values at each state u, assigned in the by-now familiar way. A conditional

$A \to B$ with truth-functional antecedent and consequent will be assigned a value one for "assertible" or zero for "nonassertible" for the model as a whole, and we will write $U \vDash A \to B$ to indicate that the value is one rather than zero. (It will then be hard to avoid slipping into reading "$U \vDash A \to B$" as "$A \to B$ holds in U." Officially "holding" here must be understood in terms of assertibility rather than truth.) The intent in framing the definition of $\vDash$ is that it should be a formal implementation of the heuristic idea (29).

Before giving the definition, something needs to be said about what properties $\leq$ ought to be assumed to have. The pertinent properties are listed here. In each case it is understood that the property specified is to hold for *all u, v, w.*

(30) *reflexivity* $u \leq u$
(31) *transitivity*   if $u \leq v$ and $v \leq w$, then $u \leq w$
(32) *totality* $u \leq v$ or $v \leq u$
(33) *antisymmetry*   if $u \leq v$ and $v \leq u$, then $u = v$

Given that $\leq$ is supposed to be a *nonstrict comparative* relation, reflexivity and transitivity are obvious requirements and will be assumed without comment. The status of totality and antisymmetry is not so obvious.

Now how to implement the heuristic idea (29)? In a finite total, antisymmetric model, there will be, among all A-states, or states where A is true, a unique A-state u of minimum remoteness, having $u \leq v$ for all other A-states v. It is natural in that case to define $U \vDash A \to B$ to hold iff B is true in this state of minimum remoteness. In a finite total but non-antisymmetric model, there may be several A-states $u_0, u_1, \ldots$ all tied for the title of state of minimum remoteness, *all* having $u_i \leq v$ for all A-states v. In that case, we must take $U \vDash A \to B$ to hold iff B is true at *all* these states of minimum remoteness. In a finite nontotal model there may be no A-state of minimum remoteness, but several incomparable ones $u_0, u_1, \ldots$ of minimal remoteness, meaning that while we may not have $u_i \leq v$ for all A-states v, we at least do not have $v < u_i$ for any A-state v. In that case, we must take $U \vDash A \to B$ to hold iff B is true at *all* these states of minimal remoteness.

So far, so good, but when we come to infinite models things get trickier. Even in a total, antisymmetric model there may be no A-state of minimal remoteness, but just an infinite sequence of ever less remote ones, … $u_3 < u_2 < u_1 < u_0$. Experience has shown the following definition for $U \vDash A \to B$ to be optimal:

(34)   for every A-state u there is an A-state $v \leq u$ such that every A-state $w \leq v$ is a B-state

For finite models (34) works out to be equivalent to the definitions given earlier. This definition happens (like the convention of counting $\pi(B \mid A) = 1$ when $\pi(A) = 0$) to give $U \vDash A \to B$ when A is impossible and there are no A-states.

Then for a class of frames $\mathbf{F}$ an argument from conditional premises $A_i \to B_i$ to a conditional conclusion $C \to D$ counts as *model-theoretically valid*, and the premises as *model-theoretically implying* or having as a *model-theoretic consequence* the conclusion, iff for all models U with $(U, \leq)$ in $\mathbf{F}$, if $U \vDash A_i \to B_i$ for all i, then $U \vDash C \to D$. When used without qualification, "model-theoretic validity" will mean validity relative to the *widest* class of frames we have been considering, reflexive and transitive frames; "model-theoretic countervalidity" will mean invalidity relative to the *narrowest* class, finite, reflexive, transitive, total, antisymmetric frames. As on the probabilistic approach, hypothetical syllogism and *a fortiori* and contraposition turn out to be invalid and indeed countervalid.

Counterexamples. In each case we need only a model with two states $u < v$, one less remote than the other. For (16), let p fail at u and hold at v, q hold at both u and v, and r hold at u and fail at v. Then the least remote p-state v is a q-state, and the least remote q-state u is an r-state, but the least remote p-state v is *not* an r-state. For (17), let p hold at both u and v, q fail at u and hold at v, and r hold at u and fail at v. Then the least remote p-state u is an r-state, but the least remote $(p \wedge q)$-state v is not an r-state. For (18), let p hold at both u and v, and q fail at u and hold at v. Then the least remote p-state u is a $\neg q$-state, but the least remote q-state v is not a $\neg p$-state.

4.5 Conditional Deductions

The probabilistic and model-theoretic approaches can be complemented by some notion of demonstration or deduction. Since we are concerned only with arguments whose premises and conclusions are indicative conditionals between truth-functional compounds, there can be no forming of leading principles and reduction of questions about deducibility to questions about demonstrability. So the format for proof procedures will have to be a little different from that used so far.

Certain axioms and primitive rules will be adopted, and then a *deduction* of conclusion $C \to D$ from premises $A_i \to B_i$ will be a sequence of conditionals, each of which is either *one of the premises* or an axiom or follows from earlier ones by a rule, and the last of which is the conclusion. The conclusion is *deducible* from the premises iff there is a deduction of it. The primitive rules can themselves be stated as saying certain conclusions are deducible from certain premises, and the axioms as saying that certain conclusions are deducible from (any or) no premises at all.

The symbol for deducibility will be $\vdash$. The axiom and rules are then these:

(35) $\vdash A \to B$ if $A \supset B$ is a tautology

(36a) $A \to B, A \to C \vdash (A \wedge B) \to C$

(37a) $A \to B, (B \wedge A) \to C \vdash A \to C$

(38a) $A \to C, B \to C \vdash (A \vee B) \to C$

A host of other deducibilities then follow in short order:

(36b) $A \to B, A \to C \vdash (B \wedge A) \to C$

(37b) $A \to B, (A \wedge B) \to C \vdash A \to C$

(38b) $A \to C, B \to C \vdash (B \vee A) \to C$

(39) $A \to B \vdash A \to B'$ if $B \supset B'$ is a tautology

(40a) $A \to A', A' \to A, A \to B \vdash A' \to B$

(40b) $A \to B \vdash A' \to B$ if $A \supset A'$ and $A' \supset A$ are tautologies

(41a) $A \to (B \wedge C) \vdash A \to B$

(41b) $A \to B, A \to C \vdash A \to (B \wedge C)$

(41c) $A \to B_1, \dots, A \to B_n \vdash A \to C$
       if C is a tautological consequence of $B_1, \dots, B_n$

(42) $A \to C, B \to D \vdash (A \vee B) \to (C \vee D)$

Proofs. For (39) note that if $B \supset B'$ is a tautology, so is $(B \wedge A) \supset B'$, and we have $(B \wedge A) \to B'$ by (35) and from this and $A \to B$ there follows $A \to B'$ by (37a). For (40a), from $A \to A'$ and $A \to B$ there follows $(A \wedge A') \to B$ by (36a) and from this and $A' \to A$ there follows $A' \to B$ by (37a). (35) and (40a) yield (40b), which with (36a), (37a), (38a) yields (36b), (37b), (38b). Henceforth (36), (37), (38) will be cited without distinguishing the (a) and (b) versions. For (41a), $((B \wedge C) \wedge A) \to B$ follows by (35), and from this and $A \to (B \wedge C)$ there follows $A \to B$ by (37). For (41b), from $A \to B$ and $A \to C$ there follows $(A \wedge B) \to C$ by (36), while $((A \wedge B \wedge C) \to (B \wedge C)$ follows by (35), and from these $(A \wedge B) \to (B \wedge C)$ follows by (37) and from this and $A \to B$ there follows $A \to (B \wedge C)$ by (37). For (42), $A \to C$ and $B \to D$ give $A \to (C \vee D)$ and $B \to (C \vee D)$ by (39), and these give $(A \vee B) \to (C \vee D)$ by (38). The proof of (41c), which subsumes (41a) and (41b), is left to the reader.

The deduction procedure is sound and complete both for the probabilistic and for the model-theoretic notions of validity of arguments, which therefore agree; moreover, there is a decision procedure. The key to the proof is a technical notion introduced in the next section.

4.6 THE ADAMS TEST

The argument from a set S of premises $A_i \to B_i$ to a conclusion $C \to D$ is said to *ace the Adams test* iff the disjunction of all the antecedents A_i and C has as a tautological consequence the disjunction of all $(A_i \wedge \neg B_i)$ and $(C \wedge D)$. It is said to *pass the Adams test* if the argument from some subset S' of the premise set S to the conclusion aces the Adams test; otherwise it *fails the Adams test*. It is decidable whether an argument passes the Adams test, since tautological consequence is decidable.

What can then be proved is the following pair of theorems:

---

(43) *Soundness*: If an argument passes the Adams test, then the conclusion is deducible from the premises, and the argument is both probabilistically and model-theoretically valid.

(44) *Completeness*: If an argument fails the Adams test, then the conclusion is not deducible from the premises, and the argument is both probabilistically and model-theoretically countervalid.

Proving these theorems easily reduces to proving the following five lemmas:

(45) If the conclusion of an argument is deducible from the premises,
then the argument is model-theoretically valid.

(46) If an argument aces the Adams test,
then its conclusion is deducible from its premises.

(47) If an argument aces the Adams test,
then its conclusion is a probabilistic consequence of its premises.

(48) If an argument fails the Adams test,
then it is model-theoretically countervalid.

(49) If an argument fails the Adams test,
then it is probabilistically countervalid.

Proofs. For (45) we assume that there is a deduction of the conclusion $C \to D$ from premises $A_i \to B_i$ and that each premise holds in the model U, and prove that each line of the deduction, including the conclusion, holds in U. This requires showing that the conditional in (35) holds in U, and that in each of (36a)–(38a), if the two-premise conditionals of the rule hold in U, so does the conclusion conditional. For (35), we simply note that if $A \supset B$ is a tautology, then B is true in *every* state in which A is true, that *every* A-state is a B-state, and we do not even need to recall the details of the complicated definition (*) of $\vDash$. For (36a) we do need to recall it. Suppose $A \to B$ and $A \to C$ hold in U, to prove $(A \wedge B) \to C$ holds in U. Well, for every $(A \wedge B)$-state u, since u is in particular an A-state, and $A \to B$ holds in U,

87

there is an A-state $v \leq u$ such that *every* A-state $w \leq v$ is a B-state, and the $(A \wedge B)$-states $\leq v$ coincide with the A-states $\leq v$. And since v is an A-state and $A \rightarrow C$ holds in U, there is an A-state $v' \leq v$ such that every A-state $w \leq v'$ is a C-state. Since the A-states $\leq v$ coincide with the $(A \wedge B)$-states $\leq v$, we have shown that for every $(A \wedge B)$-state u there is an $(A \wedge B)$-state $v' \leq u$ such that every $(A \wedge B)$-state $w \leq v'$ is a C-state, which is what it means for $(A \wedge B) \rightarrow C$ to hold in U, which is what was to be proved. (37a) and (38a) are similar, and are left to the reader.

For (46), in the one-premise case the proof goes as follows. Let E be $(A \wedge \neg B) \vee (C \wedge D)$. The assumption that the Adams test is aced means that $(A \vee C) \supset E$ is a tautology. This gets our deduction going.

i	$A \vee C \rightarrow E$	35
ii	$A \rightarrow B$	premise
iii	$A \wedge B \rightarrow E \supset (C \wedge D)$	35
iv	$A \rightarrow E \supset (C \wedge D)$	ii, iii, 37
v	$\neg A \wedge C \rightarrow E \supset (C \wedge D)$	35
vi	$A \vee (\neg A \wedge C) \rightarrow E \supset (C \wedge D)$	iv, v, 38
vii	$A \vee C \rightarrow E \supset (C \wedge D)$	vi, 40
viii	$A \vee C \rightarrow C \wedge D$	i, vii, 41
ix	$A \vee C \rightarrow C$	viii, 39
x	$A \vee C \rightarrow D$	viii, 39
xi	$C \rightarrow A \vee C$	35
xii	$C \rightarrow D$	ix, x, xi, 40

The generalization to the many-premise case essentially consists in performing the same sort of maneuver over and over. The proof of the two-place case would suffice to illustrate all the complexities involved; it is left to the reader.

For (47), in the two-premise case the proof goes as follows. Let E be $(A_1 \wedge \neg B_1) \vee (A_2 \wedge \neg B_2) \vee (C \wedge D)$ and let F be $A_1 \vee A_2 \vee C$. The assumption that the Adams test is aced means that $F \supset E$ is a tautology. Therefore for any probability function π we have $\pi(E) \geq \pi(F)$ and $\pi(E)/\pi(F) \geq 1$. The laws of probability calculus then tell us the following:

$$(1 - \pi(B_1 \mid A_1)) + (1 - \pi(B_2 \mid A_2)) + \pi(D \mid C) =$$
$$\pi(A_1 \wedge \neg B_1)/\pi(A_1) + \pi(A_2 \wedge \neg B_2)/\pi(A_2)$$
$$+ \pi(C \wedge D)/\pi(C) \geq$$
$$\pi(A_1 \wedge \neg B_1)/\pi(F) + \pi(A_2 \wedge \neg B_2)/\pi(F)$$
$$+ \pi(C \wedge D)/\pi(F) \geq$$
$$\pi(E)/\pi(F) \geq 1$$

It follows that

$$(1 - \pi(B_1 \mid A_1)) + (1 - \pi(B_2 \mid A_2)) \geq 1 - \pi(D \mid C)$$

as required for probabilistic consequence. Generalization to the many-premise case is easy.

For (48), the assumption that the Adams test is failed implies that for every subset S of the set of premises there is an assignment $V[S]$ of truth values to sentence letters that (i) either makes C true or makes A_i true for one of the premises $A_i \to B_i$ that is in S, and (ii) makes $C \wedge D$ false and makes $A_i \wedge \neg B_i$ false for each of those premises, so that if C is true, D is false, and if A_i is true, B_i is true.

Let S_0 be the whole set of premises, and let $V_0 = V[S_0]$. If V_0 does not make C true, it must make the antecedent A_i true for one of the premises in S_0. Let S_1 be the set, necessarily smaller than S_0, of premises $A_i \to B_i$ in S_0, such that V_0 makes A_i false, and let $V_1 = V[S_1]$. If V_1 does not make C true, it must make the antecedent A_i true for one of the premises in S_1. Let S_2 be the set, necessarily smaller than S_1, of premises $A_i \to B_i$ in S_1, such that V_1 makes A_i false, and let $V_2 = V[S_2]$. Continue in this way until a V_n is obtained that makes C true (as must happen, since we eventually run out of A_i).

Introduce a finite, reflexive, transitive, total, antisymmetric model U with $n + 1$ states $u_0 < u_1 < u_2 < \ldots < u_n$, and with the sentence letters having at u_m the values assigned by V_m. Each premise $A_i \to B_i$ remains in the successive S_m so long as the antecedent A_i is valued false. The first time (if any) V_m makes A_i true, it also makes B_i true by (ii). This shows that $U \vDash A_i \to B_i$. But for the conclusion $C \to D$ the antecedent C is made true for the first time by V_n, which makes D false by (ii). So we do not have $U \vDash C \to D$, and the argument is model-theoretically countervalid.

For (49), suppose we have, as per (48), a finite, reflexive, transitive, total, antisymmetric model U with $n + 1$ states $u_0 < u_1 < u_2 < \ldots < u_n$, and with each sentence letter p having at u_m the value $V_m(p)$, in which each premise $A_i \to B_i$ holds but the conclusion $C \to D$ fails, and let any $\varepsilon > 0$ be given. Define a probability function π on formulas as follows. For each formula E, the probability $\pi(E)$ is to be this sum:

$$V_0(E) \cdot (1 - \varepsilon) + V_1(E) \cdot \varepsilon(1 - \varepsilon) + V_2(E) \cdot \varepsilon^2(1 - \varepsilon)$$
$$+ \ldots + V_n(E) \cdot \varepsilon^n$$

Then for a conditional $E \to F$ holds in the model iff $V_m(E \wedge F) = V_m(F) = 1$ for the first m such that $V_m(E) = 1$. In that case, $\pi(E \wedge F)$ is at least $\varepsilon^m(1 - \varepsilon)$ and $\pi(E)$ is at most ε^m, so $\pi(F \mid E) = \pi(E \wedge F)/\pi(E)$ is at least $1 - \varepsilon$. $E \to F$ fails in the model iff $V_m(E \wedge F) = V_m(F) = 0$ for the first m such that $V_m(E) = 1$. In that case $\pi(E \wedge F)$ is at most ε^{m+1} and $\pi(E)$ is at least $\varepsilon^m(1 - \varepsilon) + \pi(E \wedge F)$, so setting $\pi(E \wedge F) = \varepsilon^{m+1} - \delta$, where $\delta \geq 0$, $\pi(E)$ is at least $\varepsilon^m - \delta$ and $\pi(E \wedge F)/\pi(E) \leq (\varepsilon^{m+1} - \delta)/(\varepsilon^m - \delta) \leq \varepsilon$. Since the premises hold in the model, they have probability $\geq 1 - \varepsilon$, and since the conclusion fails it has probability $\leq \varepsilon$, as required for probabilistic countervalidity. Applying this method of transforming model-theoretic into probabilistic counterexamples to the model-theoretic counterexamples to hypothetical syllogism, *a fortiori*, and contraposition in section 4.4, produces the probabilistic counterexamples in section 4.3.

4.7 CONVENTIONAL IMPLICATURE

Have we found the correct logic of indicative conditionals? The results obtained so far should be very satisfying to the idealist or nihilist, but some of the ideas developed along the way suggest a line of defense of materialism. Before developing it, mention must be made of a companion to the Gricean theory of conversational implicature that has played a role in later debates, the *Gricean theory of conventional implicature*. The stock example of the phenomenon of conventional implicature is provided by the difference between "but" and "and." It is generally accepted that "*A* but *B*" differs from "*A* and *B*" by suggesting that the speaker takes there to be a *contrast* of some sort or other between *A* and *B*.

Conventional implicatures are supposed to have two main features. On the one hand, whereas a conversational implicature is not built into the meaning of an expression, and can be canceled by the speaker, a conventional implicature *is* built into the meaning of the expression and can*not* be canceled by the speaker. Thus "*A* or *B*, and I know which but I'm not telling" can be a sensible thing to say, whereas "*A* but *B*, though there is no contrast of any sort between the two" cannot. On the other hand, conventional implicature is supposed to be a dimension of meaning affecting assertibility but not truth value. That there is a contrast between poverty and honesty is not part of what has to be true in order for "She's poor but honest" to be true, as if it were a third conjunct added onto "She's poor and she's honest." If it were such a conjunct, the suggestion that there is a contrast would go away as soon as assertion is replaced by questioning or denial. But it does not. Anyone who takes offense at "She's poor but honest" on the grounds that the rich are at least as likely to be dishonest as the poor will equally take offense at "Is she poor but honest?" and "She isn't poor but honest." (Scott Soames remarks that one perhaps after all *could* say, "She's not poor *but* honest, since there's no contrast between poverty and honesty," but then he adds that this surely is best regarded as an instance of what is often called *metalinguistic negation,* comparable to "He isn't *smart*. He's brilliant." and "It isn't *ee*conomics, it's economics.")

Now it will not do for the materialist to attempt to disarm critics by claiming that $A \rightarrow B$ is true under exactly the same conditions as $A \supset B$, but differs from it in another dimension of meaning in that "if" carries a conventional implicature that makes $A \rightarrow B$ assertible under just the conditions proposed by some rival to the classical theory, such as the Adams criterion. For such a proposal would be radically incomplete. In stock examples of conventional implicature, the implicature is something present in affirmation and denial, in declarative and interrogative and imperative uses alike. The kind of proposal being contemplated only tells us what effect the presence of the supposed conventional implicature of "if" is supposed to have in the case of assertion. To complete the proposal it would have to be said what the hypothetical conventional implicature *is* (in a way allowing it to be worked out what the effect of its presence is in other "speech acts").

Some of the ideas developed in connection with the model-theoretic approach suggest a candidate. It has been said that the standard of how remote from credibility a possibility must be before it can be neglected may shift from one situation to another, but it seems in fact that the cutoff may change even within the course of a single conversation. If so, then there are *two* reasons why we may change our mind about whether a given possibility is so remote and unlikely as to be negligible. We might change our mind about the likelihood of the possibility, or we might change our mind about how unlikely a possibility has to be before we can neglect it.

Especially when engaged in contingency planning we tend to consider successively less and less likely possibilities, though some remain to the end too unlikely to be worth considering. A simple dialogue will illustrate the point:

> Y: What if it rains?
> X: Then we'll hold the party under the big tent.
> Y: But what if it rains hailstones?
> X: We'll still hold the party under the big tent. It's a sturdy tent.
> Y: But what if it rains *frogs*, and they hop in under the tent?
> X: Be serious.

Thus the full story about assertibility is not told by such criteria as (27) and (29). The full story would require an account of standards and cutoffs.

Now one candidate for a conventional implicature "if *A*..." might be that *A* is a *serious* possibility. The generally accepted view about "but" amounts to this, that the parenthetical phrase in "*A*, but (by contrast) *B*" is redundant. The candidate proposal about "if" amounts to this, that the parenthetical phrase in "if (as may be) *A*, *B*" is also redundant. According to the proposal contemplated, if we make an assertion or raise a question "if A, ... ," and A does not count as a serious possibility by the standards currently in force, then we must adjust our standards so that it does. If our interlocutor makes a conditional assertion or raises a conditional question that would require an adjustment we are unwilling to make, then we must dismiss the assertion or question, as X dismissed Y's question about frogs in the dialogue.

This implicature together with (28) can yield (29), if the notion of serious possibility is understood the right way. Namely, it must be so understood that the possibility that A is a serious possibility iff only possibilities remote relative to the possibility that A count as remote enough to be safely neglected. With that understanding, the gap between the materialist criterion and the Adams criterion is bridged. There is conformity to the Adams criterion, not because the materialist criterion is *abandoned in favor of* the Adams criterion, but rather because the implicature forces an adjustment of standards that results in the materialist criterion *delivering the same result as* the Adams criterion would in the instance at hand.

It will be noted that on the present proposal, with "if p then q" amounting to "either not-p (though it may be that p) or q," embedding a conditional as the antecedent of a conditional would, whereas embedding a conditional as the consequent of a conditional would not, involve a parenthetical clause inside a parenthetical clause, in a way that is hard to interpret. This may go some way towards explaining why the one kind of embedding is rare, while the other is not.

The recognition that standards can shift has an effect on the diagnosis of the (alleged) counterexamples to hypothetical syllogism and *a fortiori* and contraposition. When assenting to the first premise in (19) or to the premise in (20) or (21), one isn't taking seriously the possibility contemplated by the antecedent of the second premise in (19) or of the conclusion in (20) or (21). If one subsequently adjusts one's standards so that one *does* take these possibilities seriously, then previous assent, based on one's former standards, may need to be reconsidered. A bold materialist might wish to claim that the argument in (19), for instance, *is* valid, and serves as a *reductio ad absurdum* of an attitude that is willing to

93

assent to the first premise while treating the antecedent to the second premise as a serious possibility. Certainly the example is rather less effective if the premises are presented in reverse order.

Can a defense of materialism along such lines succeed? Before the present proposal or any future proposal could be really convincing, it would have to be checked against the vast range of examples of usage of indicative conditionals that have accumulated in the literature during decades of debate. Doubtless even in the most favorable outcome there would be found to be a need for some additions and amendments. (For instance, something would have to be said about conditionals of the type, "If it rains frogs, I'll eat my hat," where the point of the utterance seems to be precisely to indicate that the antecedent *shouldn't be* treated as a serious possibility.) But the task of surveying such examples is well beyond the scope of this book.

4.8 COUNTERFACTUAL CONDITIONALS

So we leave the classical theory of when $\rightarrow$ is true (namely, under the same conditions as $\supset$) confronting a rival theory of when $\rightarrow$ is assertible that is usually presented in the literature in quantitative, probabilistic form, based on the notion of subjective credence (as in section 4.3), but that in this book has also been presented in qualitative, model-theoretic form, based on the notion of degree of remoteness of epistemic possibilities from credibility (as in section 4.4).

We turn to theories of when $\Rightarrow$ is true. The modal theory (that $\Rightarrow$ is true under the same conditions as $\supset$) confronts a theory of when $\Rightarrow$ is true that perhaps also might be presented in either of two ways. It might perhaps be presented in quantitative, probabilistic form, like the presentation in section 4.3 except for substituting a notion of objective chance for the notion of subjective credence. But in the literature so far it always has been presented in qualitative, model-theoretic form, like the presentation in section 4.4 except for substituting a notion of degree of remoteness of metaphysical possibilities from reality for the notion of degree of remoteness of epistemic possibilities from credibility.

In the counterfactual case, it was early suggested that "more remote from reality" does not have to be taken as a primitive, intuitive notion, but can be analyzed in terms of a more familiar notion as amounting to "less similar to reality." It was very soon recognized, however, that we cannot equate the remoteness of a possible state of the world from the real or actual state of the world with its dissimilarity to the actual state of the world on any simple, straightforward notion of overall similarity.

The stock example concerns the possibility of some mentally unstable national leader during the Cold War period "pushing the button" and bringing about a nuclear holocaust. Many feel that this was at times very close to happening, and not a remote possibility at all, though it would have left the world in a state very dissimilar to its actual state. By contrast, most feel that the possibility of the button's being pushed but disaster averted by the electrical signal being magically or miraculously interrupted on the way from the presidential office to the missile silos is a very remote one indeed, though it might have left the world in a state virtually indistinguishable from its actual state.

It is now generally recognized that if the similarity idea can be made to work at all, it will have to involve a carefully weighted average of a carefully selected set of "respects" of similarity. It seems inappropriate, therefore, to call remoteness models "similarity models" (or "similarity semantics") as is often done in the literature, as if the basic idea of analyzing counterfactuals in terms of remoteness from reality could not be separated from the speculative idea of analyzing remoteness in terms of dissimilarity.

Now hypothetical syllogism and *a fortiori* and contraposition hold for the strict $\Rightarrow$ as well as for the material $\supset$. The same kinds of counterexamples are used to argue that they fail for counterfactuals as were used to argue that they fail for indicatives. In place of (19)–(21) pertaining to an election that is (as of the time of this writing) yet to come, we have the following, pertaining to an election now past:

(50)   If McCain had won the primary, Bush would have come in second.

If Bush had died before the primary, McCain would have won it.

So, if Bush had died before the primary, he would have come in second.

(51)   If McCain had been on the general election ballot, the Republicans would have won.

So, if McCain and Bush had both been on the general election ballot, the Republicans would have won.

(52)   If Gore had won, he wouldn't have won by a landslide.

So, if Gore had won by a landslide, he wouldn't have won.

If there are grounds for reservations about such examples, they are the same as the grounds for reservations already noted in connection with the indicative examples, involving shifts in standards as to how remote possibilities have to be before they can be neglected.

4.9 WEAK CONDITIONALS

Conjunctions aside, and the "if A, and if B, then C" construction, there are few uncontentious examples of conditionals embedded in other logical constructions. In particular, it is contentious whether conditionals have negations, and whether "it is not the case that if A, B" has any clear meaning. Certainly conditionals can be *rejected*, but they can be rejected in (at least) two ways, whether indicatives or counterfactuals, thus:

(53)   If Clinton runs, she'll win.
(54)   If Clinton runs, she won't win.
(55)   If Clinton runs, she may not win.
(56)   If Giuliani had run, he would have won.
(57)   If Giuliani had run, he would not have won.
(58)   If Giuliani had run, he might not have won.

It is contentious whether (54) or (55) or neither amounts to the negation of (53), and whether (57) or (58) or neither amounts to the negation of (56).

The view that takes (58) to be equivalent to the negation of (56) is quite popular, while the corresponding view of (55) and (53) is less so. This may be because the parallelism is imperfect, and "if A, it may be that B" is really the negation of "if A, it will be that B" where "will" is epistemic, not temporal. (This sense of "will" is illustrated when the doorbell rings and X says "That will be Smith." If Y replies "What do you mean 'will be'? Surely it already either is Smith or it isn't," then Y has mistaken an epistemic for a temporal "will.")

The weak type of conditionals occurring in (55) and (58) may be symbolized $\lozenge\rightarrow$ and $\lozenge\Rightarrow$. Extensions of the probabilistic logic of indicatives to take in negated indicatives have been proposed, with the proponents sometimes identifying these with $\lozenge\rightarrow$ conditionals. The probabilistic condition for the extended logic is not easily described in a short space. Extensions of the model-theoretic logic of counterfactuals to take in $\lozenge\Rightarrow$ conditionals have been proposed, with the proponents often identifying these with the negations of counterfactuals. The model-theoretic condition for the extended logic is just this, that $A \lozenge\Rightarrow B$ holds iff $A \Rightarrow \neg B$ fails. (The proponents of such logics generally write $\square\rightarrow$ and $\lozenge\rightarrow$ for $\Rightarrow$ and $\lozenge\Rightarrow$.)

The conditions of totality and antisymmetry now turn out to make a difference. (The extended probabilistic logic turns out to agree with the extended model-theoretic logic with totality but without antisymmetry.) At least for finite models, with both conditions assumed, $A \lozenge\Rightarrow B$ implies $A \Rightarrow B$. In finite models, with both conditions assumed there is a *unique* least remote A-state, and if it is a B-state $A \Rightarrow B$ holds, and if it is a $\neg B$-state even $A \lozenge\Rightarrow B$ fails. Without antisymmetry there can be several minimally remote A-states, and if some are and some aren't B-states, $A \lozenge\Rightarrow B$ but not $A \Rightarrow B$ holds.

A more obscure example distinguishes models with totality (but perhaps without antisymmetry) from models without totality: $(A \vee B) \Rightarrow \neg A$ and $(A \vee C) \lozenge\Rightarrow A$ imply $(B \vee C) \Rightarrow \neg C$. This principle holds for total models, and can fail in others, but the verification is left to the reader.

Evidently, there is more to the technical side of the subject than there has been space to expound here. The corresponding statements about the philosophical and linguistic sides are even more true. It may be said, however, that many of the debates on these sides of the question (for instance, over whether it is good English to reword "In order for her to have arrived by eleven, she would have to have left by nine" as "If she had arrived by eleven, she would have left by nine," or over whether, in answering such a question as "If she had arrived by eleven, what would have happened?" one may or must "backtrack" and take into account what would have to have been the case in order for the antecedent to have been the case) have few or no implications for the formal *logic* of conditionals, however important they may be for such issues as whether causation can be analyzed in terms of conditionals, and the like.

4.10 FURTHER READING

The comprehensive survey Bennett (2003), besides making original contributions of its own, evenhandedly and nonpolemically covers the philosophical and many other contributions of the greatest variety of writers: Ernest Adams on the probabilistic theory of indicatives, Robert Stalnaker and David Lewis on the remoteness theory of counterfactuals, and work on intuitive interpretation and assertability and assertibility of Anthony Appiah (nihilism), Dorothy Edgington (semi-nihilism), H. P. Grice (conversational implicature), Frank Jackson (conventional implicature), and others. Technical material, except for the trivialization theorem and improvements by Alan Hájek and others, is less thoroughly covered. Here the highly readable original books Adams (1975) and Lewis (1986) are recommended, indeed, remain indispensable. For a shorter survey by a notable contributor, see Edgington (2001). Burgess (1981b) provides completeness proofs for systems that allow embedding of conditionals inside conditionals, as the present chapter does not. Probability logic as a separate subject is treated in Hailperin (1996); integrating this material with the Adams theory of conditionals remains a task for the future.

Relevantistic Logic

5.1 THE LEWIS DEDUCTION

Objections have been raised against the classical treatment of logical implication or logical consequence for counting B as an implication or consequence of $A_1, \ldots, A_n$ in two degenerate cases: first, the case where B is valid (*ex quolibet verum*), and second, the case where the A_i are jointly unsatisfiable (*ex falso quodlibet*). Often in discussions of this issue the word "entailment" is used as a synonym for "logical implication" or "logical consequence." The instance of *ex falso quodlibet* according to which an arbitrary conclusion B is entailed by the premise $A \wedge \neg A$ (or the premises A and $\neg A$) has been found especially counterintuitive by critics. Any logic that, like those to be described in this chapter, does not count everything as following from a contradiction is called *paraconsistent*.

Now there is a deduction of medieval vintage (named, however, the *Lewis deduction* after its modern reviver, C. I. Lewis, the founder of modern modal logic) showing that one cannot give it up without giving up some other principle of great importance.

i	A	Premise
ii	$\neg A$	Premise
iii	$A \vee B$	from i
iv	B	from ii, iii

There would seem to be just two options, to give up *disjunction introduction*, according to which a disjunction follows from either of its disjuncts, or *disjunctive syllogism*, according to which from a disjunction and the negation of one of its disjuncts there follows the other disjunct. The latter principle is sometimes called the *dog*, after the ancient claim (attributed by Sextus Empiricus to Chrysippus) that even a dog uses this form of inference when it

comes to a fork in the road, sniffs down one branch, and not finding the scent there immediately takes off down the other branch,
without stopping to sniff.

But though there appear to be just these two options, there is
in fact a third, more radical one, that of denying the *transitivity of
entailment*, the principle that if premises entail intermediate steps
which in turn entail a conclusion, then the initial premises entail that same final conclusion. Thus some have held that $A \wedge \neg A$
entails $(A \vee B) \wedge \neg A$, which in turn entails B, without $A \wedge \neg A$
entailing B.

Those who took the line of rejecting disjunctive syllogism originally called their alternative logic "relevance logic." Later some of
them took to calling it "relevant logic," so as to be able to call classical logic "irrelevant logic." Though the relevance/relevant label
is by rights a trademark of those who reject disjunctive syllogism,
that trademark has sometimes been infringed by advocates of
other options. Here "relevantistic" will be used as a legitimate label
covering all three options, and one that avoids the need to choose
between the (mainly American) "relevance" and the (mainly Aus-
tralian) "relevant" labels, and that parallels the label for the older
logic to be considered in the next chapter (which is called neither
"intuition logic" nor "intuitive logic" but "intuitionistic logic"). To
begin with we will be concerned with relevantistic theories of entailment between truth-functional formulas.

5.2 Relatedness Logic

But before considering alternatives to classical logic, let us consider an extension of classical logic, *topic* logic. In topic logic
there are three additional two-place connectives _ and \ and /,
where $A \_ B$ and $A \setminus B$ and A / B are intended to symbolize that
the subject matter of A overlaps, or is contained in, or contains
the subject matter of B.

A model for topic logic is a pair (V, W) where V assigns sentence letters truth values and W assigns sentence letters subsets
of some set T, thought of as the set of topics. For compound formulas $W(\neg A) = W(A)$ and $W(A \$ B) = W(A) \cup W(B)$ for any

two-place connective §, while V works the classical way with $\neg$ and $\wedge$ and $\vee$, and we have

(1) $V(A \_ B) = 1$ iff $W(A) \cap W(B) \neq \varnothing$
(2) $V(A \setminus B) = 1$ iff $W(A) \subseteq W(B)$
(3) $V(A / B) = 1$ iff $W(B) \subseteq W(A)$

Writing $A \supset B$ for $\neg A \vee B$, we write $A \supseteq B$ for $(A \supset B) \wedge (A \_ B)$ and $A \setminus\supset B$ for $(A \supset B) \wedge (A \setminus B)$ and $A \supset\!/ B$ for $(A \supset B) \wedge (A / B)$.

A formula is valid if it comes out true in all models. It is easily seen that in any model $W(A)$ is simply the union of the $W(p_i)$ for the sentence letters p_i occurring in A. It follows that if A and B are classical formulas without the new connectives, then $A \supseteq B$ or $A \setminus\supset B$ or $A \supset\!/ B$ is valid iff A classically entails B and the set of sentence letters occurring in A overlaps with or is contained in or contains the set of sentence letters occurring in B, as the case may be.

The classical doctrine is that premises A_i entail conclusion B iff $A \supset B$ is valid, where A is the conjunction of the A_i. One can now imagine three heresies, namely, those requiring the validity instead of $A \supseteq B$ or of $A \setminus\supset B$ or of $A \supset\!/ B$. There have been real-life advocates of the first two of the three. The first is the view known in the literature as "relatedness logic"; the second is part of the view known in the literature as "analytic implication"; the third might be called "co-analytic implication." All three count a multiple-premise argument as valid if the single-premise argument whose premise is the conjunction of the multiple premises, and whose conclusion is the same, is valid.

It is easily seen that entailment in analytic and co-analytic implication are transitive. It is easily seen that the argument from p to $p \vee q$, and the argument from $p \wedge \neg p$ to $(p \vee q) \wedge \neg p$, are valid in relatedness logic and for analytic implication, but not for co-analytic implication, while the arguments from $(p \vee q)$, $\neg p$ to q and from $(p \vee q) \wedge \neg p$ to q are valid in relatedness logic and for co-analytic implication, but not for analytic implication. Thus transitivity fails for entailment in relatedness logic, while disjunction introduction fails for analytic implication, and disjunctive syllogism for co-analytic implication.

Note that the first relatedness condition (or overlap of sets of sentence letters) is implied by the other two. It is in fact accepted as a *necessary* condition for entailment by all schools of relevantistic logicians. Now there is a classical result called the *Craig interpolation theorem* saying that unless *A* is unsatisfiable or *C* is valid, then if *A* entails *C*, there is a *B*, called an *interpolant*, such that *A* entails *B*, *B* entails *C*, and the sentence letters occurring in *B* are those that occur both in *A* and in *C*. So classically the overlap condition holds *except in the degenerate cases*. Relevantistic logicians will not allow that exception.

From the point of view of relevantistic logics with more adherents, the trio of sects under discussion err by in a sense giving *too much* importance to relevance of topic. Each either counts $A \wedge \neg A \wedge B$ as entailing $\neg B$ or counts A as entailing $\neg A \vee B \vee \neg B$ or both, simply because the argument from premise to conclusion is truth-preserving and the topic of the conclusion is appropriately related to the topic of the premise. Other relevantists reject these arguments because in neither case does the relation of topics have anything to do with *why* the argument is truth-preserving.

A doctrine common to other relevantistic logics is that a conjunction of plain and negated sentence letters entails a disjunction of plain and negated sentence letters iff some sentence letter appears in both premise and conclusion "with the same sign" (that is, both plain or both negated). This is in effect a requirement that not only is there an overlap of topic, but further, the overlap of topic is what *makes* the argument truth-preserving.

The mere existence of at least one view that rejects disjunction introduction raises the question why anyone would ever *want* to infer a disjunction from a disjunct. An unsophisticated application of Gricean theory would suggest that a disjunction is never assertable when a disjunct is. A less simplistic application would recognize that if one has grounds for believing a disjunction *beyond* whatever grounds one has for believing the disjunct, then one may have an even higher degree of belief in the disjunction than in the disjunct, even if one's degree of belief in the disjunct is rather high. Then the desideratum of informativeness, which points towards asserting the disjunct, is in tension with the desideratum of reliability, which points towards asserting the disjunction. There is no reason not to assert both. One might say, "Very likely A, and surely A or B," and indeed, one would be understood as meaning that even if one just said, "A; well, A or B."

To come up with a Gricean explanation why one might assert a disjunction when one's sole grounds for believing it are grounds for believing one of the disjuncts, one must recall that there is a third desideratum, *pertinence*. It may be that the information that the disjunction holds (that the child has an older sibling, say) is more pertinent to present purposes (evaluating some psychological generalization about birth order, say) than the information that the disjunct holds (that the child has an older brother, or that the child has an older sister).

Inference from disjunct to disjunction *for purposes of subsumption under a generalization* is extremely common in mathematics. A proof by mathematical induction of "for all n, $A(n)$ or $B(n)$" has as its first step the proof of the case $n = 0$, which is to say, the proof of disjunction "$A(0)$ or $B(0)$." And nothing is more common than for the proof of "$A(0)$ or $B(0)$" in such a context to be by inference from $A(0)$ or from $B(0)$. In mathematical practice, *disjunction introduction is indispensable*.

5.3 PERFECTIONIST LOGIC

We say that formula A *perfectly* entails formula B iff A classically entails B, *and this classical entailment is not a degenerate case*, meaning that A is satisfiable and B invalid. Both disjunction introduction (as the argument from p to $p \vee q$) and conjunction elimination (as the argument from $p \wedge q$ to p) are perfect entailments. Perfection cannot be advocated as the criterion of entailment because there are imperfect arguments that are instances of perfect ones (such as the argument from p to $p \vee \neg p$ or from $q \wedge \neg q$ to q), and any instance of a valid form of argument must be recognized as a valid form of argument.

But there are relevantistic logicians who allow *only* this exception. We say that A *perfectibly* entails B iff the argument from A to B is either perfect itself or a substitution instance of a perfect argument. Then *perfectionist* logic advocates perfectibility as the criterion of entailment. Since classical entailment is decidable (there are mechanical procedures such as doing truth tables for determining whether or not one classical formula entails another) and likewise classical satisfiability and invalidity, it is decidable whether A perfectly entails B. Since apart from relettering there are only finitely many arguments "from C to D" of which a given argument "from A to B" could be obtained by substitution, it is also decidable whether A perfectibly entails B.

Since by Craig's theorem there must be a sentence letter in common between premise and conclusion in a perfect argument, and substitution preserves this property, there must be a sentence letter in common in a perfectible argument. As the reader can verify, a conjunction of plain and negated sentence letters perfectibly entails a disjunction of plain and negated sentence letters iff some sentence letter appears in both premise and conclusion with the same sign.

The argument from p to $(p \lor q)$ is perfect. The argument from $p \land r$ to $(p \lor q) \land r$ is also perfect, so the argument from $p \land \neg p$ to $(p \lor q) \land \neg p$ is perfectible, and the argument from $(p \lor q) \land \neg p$ to q is perfect. But the argument from $p \land \neg p$ to q is *not* perfect, and the only more general form of which it is an instance is the argument from p to q, which is not even classically valid, so the argument from $p \land \neg p$ to q is *not* perfectible. So transitivity fails for perfectible entailment. (It is easily seen to hold for perfect entailment.)

The description of the most natural extension of the perfectibility criterion to multiple premise arguments requires some background. A *sequent* consists of two sequences of formulas with a turnstile between. Classically, a sequent

(4) $A_1, \dots, A_m \vdash B_1, \dots, B_n$

is counted valid iff for every assignment V of truth values to sentence letters, if V makes all the A_i true, then V makes at least one of the B_j true. (So the multiple premises are being treated conjunctively, and the multiple conclusions disjunctively.) In case $m = 0$, so that the sequence on the left is empty, and $n = 1$, validity of the sequent is equivalent to validity of that formula. In case $n = 0$, validity of the sequent is equivalent to the joint unsatisfiability the formulas on the left (or if $m = 1$, unsatisfiability of the formula on the left). The perfectionist criterion in the single-premise, single-conclusion case may be restated as requiring that $A \vdash B$ should be classically valid, but $A \vdash \varnothing$ and $\varnothing \vdash B$ should not be. The generalization is now that a sequent should be valid iff it is classically valid and no *proper subsequent*, obtained by dropping one or more formulas from one or the other or both sides, should be classically valid. One may ask whether transitivity holds for perfect entailment only in the sense that one may ask whether, if $A_1, \dots , A_m$ perfectly entail B and B perfectly entails $C_1, \dots , C_m$, then $A_1, \dots , A_m$ perfectly entail $C_1, \dots , C_m$. We leave it to the reader to answer this question.

The assumption of the transitivity of entailment seems to pervade mathematics, where axioms are used to prove lemmas, lemmas are used to prove theorems, theorems are used to prove corollaries, and on and on, and every result in the chain is held to be implied by the original axioms. It might be wondered how one could have any kind of proof procedure at all if transitivity is disallowed. But in fact there is a style of proof procedure called *sequent calculus* that seems to get around the difficulty. Instead of demonstrations, or sequences of formulas each of which is either an axiom or follows from earlier ones by a rule, we consider *sequent-demonstrations*, or sequences of sequents each of which is either a *sequent-axiom* or follows from earlier ones by a *sequent-rule*. With a sequent calculus approach, the cumulativity of mathematics is not represented by an ever-growing sequence of formulas, Axioms, then Lemmas, then Theorems, then Corollaries, but rather by an ever-growing sequence of sequents, of the form "Axioms $\vdash$ _____" where the blank is successively filled in by Axioms, then Lemmas, then Theorems, then Corollaries.

The sequent-axioms are just the sequents of the form $A \vdash A$. Classically there are a number of systems of sequent rules that will permit the demonstration of all classically valid sequents. Among rules that turn up in such systems the following four will call for comment (wherein Greek letters represent sequences of formulas):

(5) *Cut*
from $A \vdash B$ and $B \vdash C$ to infer $A \vdash C$

(6) *Thinning*
     from $\Pi \vdash \Sigma$ to infer $\Pi, A \vdash \Sigma$ or $\Pi \vdash A, \Sigma$
(7) *Left disjunction introduction*
     from $\Pi, A, B \vdash \Sigma$ to infer $\Pi, A \vee B \vdash \Sigma$
(8) *Right disjunction introduction*
     from $\Pi \vdash A, \Sigma$ or $\Pi \vdash B, \Sigma$ to infer $\Pi \vdash A \vee B, \Sigma$

Each has more general versions that need not detain us. The cut rule directly expresses the classical doctrine that entailment is transitive. Moreover, its use is indispensable if one is to get a sequent calculus demonstration that anywhere near directly formalizes mathematicians' proofs. But the cut rule is in principle dispensable in sequent calculus (if the other rules are appropriately chosen). So says a famous "metatheorem," the *Gentzen cut-elimination theorem*. Moreover, the proof not only shows that if a sequent demonstration using cut exists, one not using cut also exists, but actually shows how it is possible in principle to convert a given sequent demonstration using cut into one not using cut. The conversion, however, though possible in principle is in general not feasible in practice, since fairly short demonstrations get blown up into astronomically long ones.

The cut rule is rejected by perfectionism, and equally thinning (which leads from the perfect $A \vdash A$ into the imperfectible $A, B \vdash A$ or $A \vdash A, B$). Another metatheorem tells us, however, that (if the other rules such as left and right disjunction introduction are appropriately chosen) from a classical sequent demonstration without cut, one can extract a perfectionistically acceptable demonstration of the same sequent or a subsequent. The extraction procedure moreover does not much increase the lengths of demonstrations.

So from a mathematician's proof of a theorem from axioms, involving the assumption of the transitivity of entailment, it is in principle possible to produce a more or less direct formalization as a sequent demonstration in classical sequent calculus with cut, then to transform this into a sequent demonstration in classical sequent calculus without cut, and then to extract from that a perfectionistically acceptable sequent demonstration, if not that the original axioms entail the theorem, then either that a subset of the original axioms entail the theorem, or that the axioms entail a contradiction. In general, however, the three-step procedure is not practically feasible, the trouble coming at the second step. But if one is convinced that one's axioms are true, and therefore do not entail a contradiction, even without carrying through the procedure a perfectionist can conclude that the theorem must be true, since it is entailed by a subset of the set of axioms.

Or rather, the perfectionist could conclude this *provided the metatheorem has been proved in a perfectionistically acceptable manner.* But this it has not been, and it is doubtful if it ever will be. Thus in practice one who is really, truly, and sincerely a perfectionist cannot accept mathematicians' proofs. In mathematical practice, *transitivity of entailment is indispensable.*

5.4 RELEVANCE/RELEVANT LOGIC: "FIRST-DEGREE" FRAGMENT

Now for the account of entailments among truth-functional compounds given by relevance/relevant logic (or *r-logic* for short). This part of r-logic is called the "first-degree" fragment. Classically an entailment

(9) $(\neg)p_1 \wedge \ldots \wedge (\neg)p_m \vdash (\neg)q_1 \vee \ldots \vee (\neg)q_n$

can hold in either of two cases: (i) some sentence letter occurs on both sides with the same sign (either both plain or both negated), (ii) some sentence letter appears with both signs (both plain and negated) on the same side. Like perfectionistic logic, r-logic maintains that entailment holds only in the nondegenerate case (i).

A simple way to describe the relationship between classical and r-logical entailment in this case would be as follows. Introduce auxiliary sentence letters, so that each ordinary sentence letter p, q, r, ... has an auxiliary sentence letter p', q', r', ... as a *mate.* Replace each p_i or q_j that appears negated in (9) by its mate to obtain (9'). Then (9) holds in r-logic iff (9') holds in classical logic.

This relationship can be extended to more complex cases. We define by recursion on complexity the distinction between the positive and the negative occurrences of a sentence letter in a formula. In an atomic formula, the sentence letter occurs positively.

If § is conjunction or disjunction, the positive (respectively, negative) occurrences of a sentence letter in A § B are the positive (respectively, negative) occurrences in A and in B. The positive (respectively, negative) occurrences in $\neg A$ are the negative (respectively, positive) occurrences in A. For any formula A involving ordinary sentence letters, let A^* be the result of replacing all negative occurrences of any sentence letter by an occurrence of its auxiliary mate. Then premises $A_1, \ldots , A_n$ entail conclusion B according to r-logic iff $A_1^*, \ldots , A_n^*$ entail conclusion B^* according to classical logic.

This was not the r-logicians' original definition—that was rather more complicated—but it is equivalent. It is easily seen to follow from the present definition that r-entailment is decidable. It also follows from the present definition that r-entailment is transitive. On performing the substitution of mates, the argument from p to $p \vee q$ remains the classical valid argument from p to $p \vee q$, since all occurrences of sentence letters are positive, so in disjunction introduction the premise r-entails the conclusion. On performing the substitution of mates, the argument from $(p \vee q) \wedge \neg p$ to q becomes the classically invalid argument from $(p \vee q) \wedge \neg p'$ to q, so in disjunctive syllogism the premise does *not* r-entail the conclusion. We leave it to the reader to verify that $(p \wedge q)$ r-entails p but that $\neg(p \wedge q) \wedge p$ does not r-entail $\neg q$.

5.5 INTENSIONAL DISJUNCTION

Now inference from "A or B" and "not A" to B is so frequent in commonsense reasoning and mathematical proof that the r-logicians' rejection of disjunctive syllogism as "A simple inferential mistake such as only a dog would make" appears seriously counterintuitive. Many r-logicians used to argue that it is less counterintuitive than it seems, by distinguishing two kinds of disjunction. The claim was that though they do indeed reject inference from "$A \vee B$" and "$\neg A$" to B, commonsense and mathematical arguments from "A or B" and "not A" to B often only appear to be of this rejected form, and are really of another form r-logicians accept, namely, inference from "$A + B$" and "$\neg A$" to B, where $+$

indicates a stronger, "intensional," non-truth-functional kind of disjunction, to be distinguished from the weaker, "extensional," truth-functional kind of disjunction indicated by ∨. "$A + B$" was supposed to amount to something like "$A \vee B$ *and A and B are relevant to each other.*" Disjunctive syllogism was claimed to be valid for + and invalid for ∨. By contrast, disjunction introduction was claimed to be invalid for + and valid for ∨ (so that the Lewis deduction is a kind of fallacy of equivocation between two different senses of disjunction), since $A + B$ could be false even if one or both of the disjuncts is true, if there is no "relevant" connection between those disjuncts.

What is one to make of this claim that in commonsense, intuitive cases where one argues from "A or B" and "not A" to B, the first, disjunctive premise is something stronger than the mere truth-functional disjunction that could be inferred from either of its disjuncts? Well, it is quite true that inference from "A or B" and "not A" to B will never be useful if the sole grounds for the disjunctive premise are grounds for one of its disjuncts. For if the disjunct in question is A, then the grounds for the first premise conflict with any grounds for the second premise, and we need to reconsider, while if the disjunct in question is B, then we have the conclusion already, without the argument.

But there are cases where the disjunction was originally established by X simply by inference from a disjunct (which kind of inference, remember, is supposed to be valid only for ∨, not for +), and Y has obtained the disjunctive information from X and also has the information that the first disjunct is false, and then usefully concludes, by disjunctive syllogism, that the second disjunct is true, thus recovering information that X had but did not transmit. Whatever it is that + adds to ∨ is something X didn't have and therefore can't have transmitted to Y, so it seems Y's application of disjunctive syllogism must be regarded as an application of the version r-logicians reject. A simple instance (with X = one's former self and Y = one's present self) would be where one remembers that one knew one of the disjuncts in the past, but now needs to know, and no longer remembers, *which* disjunct. If one somehow finds out that the first disjunct is false, one can usefully conclude that the second disjunct is true.

In the wake of such examples, the story about an ambiguity in the ordinary-language "or" between two senses of disjunction is no longer very widely advocated or accepted. If it is rejected, then r-logicians cannot accept disjunctive syllogism, as encountered in commonsense reasoning and mathematicians' proofs, as a form of argument generally valid. (Some r-logicians have claimed that forms of argument that are not generally valid can somehow nonetheless be legitimately used in special situations; other r-logicians have joined classical logicians in rejecting such claims.) And though the status of toy examples is of little importance in itself, experience has shown that mathematicians' proofs cannot in general be formalized in r-logic. Since r-logicians have been caught using the forbidden principle in the proof of a metatheorem about their own logic, it is hard for them to deny that, in mathematical practice, *disjunctive syllogism is indispensable*.

5.6 APPLICATIONS OF QUADRIVALENT LOGIC

The early writings of r-logicians, the writings that founded the movement, certainly gave every appearance of having been intended as descriptive criticism: criticism of classical logic as incorrectly describing the correct practice of mathematicians and others. But if disjunction introduction, the transitivity of entailment, and disjunctive syllogism really are all three indispensable in orthodox mathematical practice, as has been claimed, then relevantistic logic fails as descriptive criticism. Two routes are then open to the relevantistic logician: the radical option of becoming a prescriptive critic, and urging a revision of mathematics; and the moderate option of (re)interpreting relevantistic logic so that it attempts to supplement rather supplant classical logic. Both routes have been taken.

The various applications of various relevantistic logics that have been suggested in the literature are many, and only two, both pertaining to the first-degree fragment of r-logic, will be mentioned briefly as examples here. Both are based on thinking of r-logic as a quadrivalent (four-valued) alternative to classical bivalent (two-valued) logic. For we may think of a model for r-logic as given by a *pair* (V, W) where V assigns values 1 or 0 to the original sentence letters, and W assigns values 1 and 0 to the auxiliary sentence letters. Then there are four possibilities for any given original sentence letter: both it and its mate are valued 1, it is valued 1 and its mate valued 0, it is valued 0 and its mate valued 1, and both it and its mate are valued 0. So the pair (V, W) may be represented by a single X assigning each of the original sentence letters one of four values $(1,1)$ or $(1, 0)$ or $(0, 1)$ or $(0, 0)$; or "true with untrue negation" or "true with true negation" or "untrue with untrue negation" or "untrue with true negation." The valuation can then be extended in a natural way from sentence letters to other formulas. Then A entails B according to r-logic iff all four-valued assignments that make A true make B true also. We leave the details to the reader.

A first example of a potential application of r-logic is to circuit design, a significant application of sentential logic touched on even in some introductory textbooks. One has a large, complex circuit with many switches that can be closed (allowing current to pass) or open (so current is blocked), and can be connected in series (so all have to be closed for current to pass) or parallel (so all have to be open for current to be blocked). The switches open and close in batches. A single master P-switch set one way closes all switches labeled p and opens all switches labeled $\neg p$, and set the other way does the opposite. A single master Q-switch similarly controls the switches labeled q and $\neg q$. And so on.

The problem is to design a circuit such that (i) for the same settings of the master switches the same result (current passing or blocked) will be obtained as for the given circuit, (ii) the circuit will contain as few switches (and therefore be of as low cost) as possible. Classical logic is applied by representing series and parallel connections as conjunction and disjunction, respectively, reducing the problem of circuit design to the problem of finding, for a given formula, another formula that (i) is logically equivalent to the given formula, and (ii) contains as few occurrences of sentence letters as possible. The problem has been of enough practical importance that a considerable literature on "shortest equivalents" has built up.

Now though the p- and $\neg p$-switches are intended to work in such a way that when the former are closed, the latter are open, and vice versa, it may happen briefly during transitions that both kinds of switches are open, or both kinds closed. This may or may not matter; it tends to matter when short-term fluctuations in the circuit can have long-term consequences. Different circuits equivalent by classical logic may have different susceptibilities to such "glitches" or "hazards," as they are called. To give a trivial example, though a simple p-switch is classically equivalent to a p-switch connected in series with a setup of a q-switch and a $\neg q$-switch connected in parallel (represented by the formula $p \wedge (q \vee \neg q)$), the latter is susceptible to the hazard of q- and $\neg q$-switches both being open and current thus blocked when the p-switch is closed and it is intended that current should pass. By contrast, different circuits will have the same hazards if they are equivalent not just by classical but by r-logic.

A second example of a proposed application of r-logic is a computer that answers questions not merely by retrieving information directly recorded in its data base, but also by drawing some simple logical inferences. Since any large database is likely to have a contradiction in it somewhere, one would not want such a computer to draw all simple logical inferences that are valid according to classical logic, since this would allow giving an arbitrary conclusion q as output if given contradictory information p and $\neg p$ as input. This is *not* in itself to say that p and $\neg p$ don't logically imply q, but only that if they do, it isn't wise to let the computer (which has no critical faculties) notice that they do. The thought that p could be called "both true and having a true negation" (respectively "neither true nor having a true negation") *according to the database* if it contains both (respectively, neither) of p and $\neg p$ suggests that the inferences it is wise to allow the computer to make would be those that are valid according to r-logic. (A variant proposal would use a three-valued logic, preventing the deduction of arbitrary conclusions from contradictions, but allowing the deduction of tautologies from arbitrary premises.)

5.7 Dialethism

Contrasting with moderate views that emphasize such applications is a more radical view that maintains that p can not merely both be true and have a true negation according to some body of information or belief, but that *p* can *literally* both be true and have a true negation. If falsity is identified with truth of negation, this means that *p* can literally be both true and false. Adherents of this view are called *dialethists*. (Some write "dialetheists," but this is like writing "economeists"; the older term "alethic," not "aletheic," shows the correct formation: the Greek suffixes -ικος and -ισμος and -ιστης, corresponding to the English -ic and -ism and -ist, attach to the root of a word, and the root here is αληθ-.)

Various supposed examples of true contradictions are cited by dialethists. It is a common view that the liar and truth-teller sentences ("This very sentence is not true" and "This very sentence is true") are instances of truth-value gaps, cases where we have neither truth nor falsehood (or truth of negation). Some dialethists cite them, rather, as examples of truth-value gluts, cases where we have both truth and falsehood (or truth of negation). One dialethist logic is simply a trivalent logic originally intended as a logic of gaps but sensationalized by being reinterpreted as a logic of gluts. More interesting is the proposal to use a quadrivalent logic, and take the liar to show a glut and the truth-teller to show a gap.

For another example, it is claimed to be true both that the Russell set (the set of all sets that are not elements of themselves) is an element of itself and that it is not. Obviously, mathematics would require revision if this particular example were accepted. It is suggested that accepting this example does not merely require a revised set theory but permits an *improved* set theory. The thought is that in place of the complicated existence axioms of orthodox set theory one can have the simple, naive axiom that *every* condition (including the condition "is not an element of itself") determines a set. One has to pay for the simplicity of the axiom by giving up certain widely used forms of argument, which threatens to hobble mathematics, but perhaps these can be made available selectively, under special circumstances. The trouble is that in specifying the circumstances all the complexity of the orthodox axioms and more is likely to re-emerge. But indeed no relevantistic alternative to orthodox mathematics has been developed to the point where it constitutes a serious rival comparable, say, to the subject of chapter 6, intuitionistic mathematics.

Chapter Five

5.8 Relevance/Relevant Logic: "Purely Implicational" Fragment

There is another side to r-logic, a theory of "implication," in a sense of "implication" weaker than *logical* implication or entailment. Though symbolized → it cannot be identified with the conditional, either, as can be seen from the r-logicians' rejection of $B \to (A \to B)$. For this principle is a self-evident one if "$A \to B$" is simply the indicative conditional (which may include "noninterference" conditionals "(even) if A, (still) B"), since surely if B is the case, then even if A is (also) the case, still B is the case. The r-logicians' → represents, perhaps, a distinctively *non*-noninterference conditional, expressible perhaps by "if A, then B *for that reason*."

Formally its properties are best introduced by contrast not with classical logic or with the kind of theories considered in chapter 4, but with the part of the logic to be considered in chapter 6, intuitionistic logic, that deals with the conditional →. Here we have two axioms, of which the first but not the second is acceptable to r-logicians:

(10) $(A \to (B \to C)) \to ((A \to B) \to (A \to C))$
(11) $A \to (B \to A)$

The only rule is modus ponens (MP). The logic with just these two axioms and just this rule is often called *positive* logic. The most basic theorem is the following:

(12) $A \to A$

Proof.

i $(A \to ((A \to A) \to A)) \to$ Ax (10)
      $((A \to (A \to A)) \to (A \to A))$
ii $A \to ((A \to A) \to A))$ Ax (11)
iii $(A \to (A \to A)) \to (A \to A)$ i, ii, MP
iv $A \to (A \to A)$ Ax (11)

(12) now follows from iii and iv by MP.

The notion of proof or demonstration has a companion notion of *proof from hypotheses* or *deduction*. A deduction (of a formula B) from formulas $A_1, \ldots, A_n$ is a sequence of steps (the last of which is B) each of which is either one of the A_i or an axiom or follows from earlier steps by the rule. We have defined B to be deducible from the A_i iff the leading principle (10) is demonstrable, but this turns out to be equivalent to the existence of a deduction of B from the A_i by repeated application of the *deduction theorem*. This theorem says that if there is a deduction of C from $A_1, \ldots, A_n, B$, then there is a deduction of $B \to C$ from $A_1, \ldots, A_n$. The axioms (10) and (11) (and the theorem (12)) are *just* what is needed (along with MP) to get the deduction theorem.

> *Proof.* It is enough to show that for each line D in the deduction of C from $A_1, \ldots, A_n, B$ there is a deduction of $B \to D$ from $A_1, \ldots, A_n$. The first line of the deduction, or any line *not* obtained from earlier lines by MP, must be B or one of the A_i or some axiom A. In the first case there is a demonstration of $B \to B$ like that which led to (12). In the second case there is a deduction of $B \to A_i$ from A_i consisting of A_i followed by the axiom $A_i \to (B \to A_i)$ followed by $B \to A_i$, which we get by MP. The third case is like the second. Now suppose we have a line D obtained by MP from lines $E \to D$ and E and have deductions of $B \to (E \to D)$ and $B \to E$ from $A_1, \ldots, A_n$. We get a deduction of $B \to D$ by adding one new line with the axiom $(B \to (E \to D)) \to ((B \to E) \to (B \to D))$, another new line with $(B \to E) \to (B \to D)$, which follows by MP, and another new line $B \to D$, which also follows by MP.

Deductions and applications of the deduction theorem may be laid out like demonstrations, but with an additional column of annotations, giving not the immediate justifications for each step, but the hypotheses on which that step ultimately depends, a notion defined as follows. An axiom depends on no hypotheses. Each hypothesis depends only on itself. A step inferred by modus ponens from two earlier steps depends on a hypothesis iff one of those earlier steps does. When the deduction theorem is applied one moves from a step C to a step $H \to C$, where H is one of the hypotheses, and deletes the number of that hypothesis from the list of dependency numbers. A line with *no* dependency numbers is then demonstrable.

Among theorems obtainable by this method, two stand out as especially significant. First we have the following:

(13) $(A \to (B \to C)) \to (B \to (A \to C))$

Proof.

i	$A \to (B \to C)$	Hyp	i
ii	B	Hyp	ii
iii	A	Hyp	iii
iv	$B \to C$	i, iii, MP	i, iii
v	C	iv, ii, MP	i, ii, iii
vi	$A \to C$	iii, v, Ded	i, ii
vii	$B \to (A \to C)$	ii, vi, Ded	i
(13)	$(A \to (B \to C)) \to (B \to (A \to C))$	i, vii, Ded	

We have written "Hyp" for hypotheses and "Ded" for applications of the deduction theorem. At line vi, for instance, C having been deduced from the three hypothesis i, ii, iii, the deduction theorem is applied to conclude that iii $\to C$ is deducible from the two hypothesis i, ii. Since the last line is deducible under *no* hypothesis, it is demonstrable, a theorem.

Similarly we have the following:

(14) $(A \to B) \to ((B \to C) \to (A \to C))$

Proof.

i	$A \to B$	Hyp	i
ii	$B \to C$	Hyp	ii
iii	A	Hyp	iii
iv	B	i, iii, MP	i, ii, iii
v	C	iv, ii, MP	i, ii, iii
vi	$A \to C$	iii, v, Ded	i, ii
vii	$(B \to C) \to (A \to C)$	ii, vi, Ded	i
(14)	$(A \to B) \to ((B \to C) \to (A \to C))$	i, vii, Ded	

It would be possible to dispense with the axioms by making application of Ded into a primitive rule. The axioms (10) and (11) could be obtained as (13) and (14) were. To obtain (11) one proceeds like this:

i	A	Hyp	i
ii	B	Hyp	ii
iii	$B \to A$	ii, i, Ded	i
iv	$A \to (B \to A)$	i, iii, Ded	

(10) can be obtained similarly, and is left to the reader.

Note that at step iii a hypothesis was discharged *that was not actually used*. This kind of maneuver the r-logician finds objectionable. One presentation of the purely implicational fragment of r-logic consists of just two rules, MP and a special version of Ded that allows the discharge of a hypothesis H to move from step C to step $H \to C$ iff the number of that hypothesis H appears among the dependency numbers of step C. All of (10), (12), (13), (14) can be obtained as theorems in this way (but not (11)). A more conventional presentation takes the four items just cited as axioms, called the *Moh-Church axioms*, and MP as the only rule. It is then possible to prove this special version of Ded.

What is to be proved is that if there is a deduction of C from $A_1, \ldots, A_n, B$ in which the number of B is among the dependency numbers for C, then there is a deduction of $B \to C$ from $A_1, \ldots, A_n$ with the dependency numbers for $B \to C$ being those for C in the old deduction, except for the number of B. The essence of the theorem is exhibited by the following simplified version. Suppose there is a deduction of C from $A_1, \ldots, A_n, B$ and we star some of its steps as follows. Axioms are not starred, hypotheses A_i are not starred, hypothesis B is starred, and if D is obtained from $E \to D$ and E, then D is starred iff at least one of $E \to D$ or E is starred. Then if C is starred, there is a deduction of $B \to C$ from $A_1, \ldots, A_n$.

> *Proof.* One shows that for each starred line D, there is a deduction of $B \to D$ from $A_1, \ldots, A_n$. There are four cases, one where (i) $D = B$, and three for modus ponens, one where (ii) $E \to D$ but not E is starred, one where (iii) not $E \to D$ but E is starred, and one where (iv) both are starred. The axioms (12), (13), (14), and (10) are exactly what are needed for each of these four cases (in the order listed). For instance, for case (i) we have $B \to B$ as an axiom. For case (ii) we suppose that since $E \to D$ is starred we have a deduction

117

of $B \to (E \to D)$, as well as a deduction of E, and we want a deduction of $B \to D$. Well, we have the axiom

(13) $(B \to (E \to D)) \to (E \to (B \to D))$

so two applications of MP will do it. The other cases use other axioms, and are left to the reader.

5.9 COMBINING THE "FIRST DEGREE" AND "PURELY IMPLICATIONAL" FRAGMENTS

Trouble comes if one tries to combine this neat system for $\to$ alone with a treatment of $\neg$ and $\wedge$ and $\vee$. For it seems that inference (*) of a conjunction from its conjuncts and (**) of a conjunct from a conjunction should be allowed, but then we would have the following deduction:

i	A	Hyp	i
ii	B	Hyp	ii
iii	$A \wedge B$	i, ii, *	i, ii
iv	A	iii, **	i, ii
v	$B \to A$	ii, iv, Ded	i
vi	$A \to (B \to A)$	i, v, Ded	

There are ways around this problem, though they appear (at least to classical logicians) *ad hoc*, and a combined r-logical system **R** produced, in which the only pure $\to$ theorems are those of the Moh-Church logic, and the only theorems of form $A \to B$ with A and B truth-functional compounds (the only first-degree theorems) are those where A r-logically entails B. The proof of this result, the *Meyer conservative extension theorem*, uses a version of Kripke models appropriate to r-logic, called *Meyer-Routley models* (another variant of Kripke models, obtained independently by Kit Fine, could also be used; both variants involve, instead of the two-place $\prec$ or $\leq$ of temporal and modal or conditional logic, a three-place relation).

One thing we often get from Kripke models in other cases is a proof of decidability. We do not in this case. For a measure of the complexity of **R** is the *Urquhart undecidability theorem*, according to which the logic is undecidable. **R** is the first and one of very few sentential logics ever advocated by anyone as correct that has turned out to be undecidable. The proof that it is so is probably the deepest in any branch of sentential logic. We have seen that the first-degree fragment is decidable, and the purely implicational fragment is, too, according to the *Kripke decidability theorem*, but the decision procedure is exceptionally complicated and well beyond the scope of this book.

One thing we sometimes get from Kripke models is a more or less natural heuristic interpretation. We get this for temporal logic and for conditional logic (in terms of time in the one case, and remoteness of possibilities in the other), as we have seen. Meyer-Routley models yield no such interpretation for r-logic, and all attempts to produce a system with models with a natural heuristic interpretation seem to lead to systems considerably different from **R**. From a movement advocating a particular system as a correction to the classical theory of what entails what, relevantism has devolved into a study of a loosely related collection of formalisms, for which various more or less technical applications are proposed.

5.10 FURTHER READING

In the interests of full disclosure it should be noted that the present author has the reputation—based on the polemical Burgess (1981c) and its sequel Burgess (1983), which includes a host of examples of everyday reasoning by disjunctive syllogism, taken from writers ranging from E. M. Curley to Saul Kripke, as well as Burgess (2005a)—of being the opposite of a friend of relevantism, so readers may find a second opinion especially desirable for the subject of this chapter. For relevance/relevant logic, the main source is the encyclopedic two-volume *Entailment* (Anderson & Belnap, 1975; Anderson, Belnap, & Dunn, 1992). The original and revised (quadrivalent) rationales for the first-degree fragment are treated, besides the controversy over intensional disjunction and the issue of the relevantists' own use of disjunctive syllogism, as well as a proposed computer-science application. The purely implicational fragment is covered from the original motivating considerations related to the deduction theorem through Kripke's decision procedure. The combined system **R** and another called **E**, Meyer-Routley and Fine models, and Urquhart's undecidability result are also discussed. There is even some coverage of minor relevantistic schools, especially analytic implication and the von Wright-Geach-Smiley precursor to perfectionist logic. The main source for perfectionism (under the label "relevant logic") is, however, Tennant (1997), where it is combined with intuitionism. For relatedness logic, see Epstein (1996). For the subsumption of relevantistic logic into a larger category containing logics whose motivation is technical, coming from linguistics and computer science (Lambek calculus, linear logic), see Restall (2000). For dialethism, see Priest (2006) and other works by the same author. For the trivalent logic of truth-value gaps, which lurks in the background, see Blamey (1986). For the distinction between descriptive and prescriptive logic, which lurks still further in the background, see Burgess (1992).

Intuitionistic Logic

6.1 MATHEMATICAL INTUITIONISM

According to classical mathematics, one can prove that there exist irrational numbers a and b such that a^b is rational as follows. Consider $\sqrt{2}^{\sqrt{2}}$. Either it is rational or it is irrational. If $\sqrt{2}^{\sqrt{2}}$ is rational, set $a = b = \sqrt{2}$, which has been known to be irrational since the earliest times. If $\sqrt{2}^{\sqrt{2}}$ is irrational, set $a = \sqrt{2}^{\sqrt{2}}$ and $b = \sqrt{2}$, and a little algebra shows $a^b = 2$, which of course is rational.

This is an example from the mathematical folklore of an existence proof of the kind called *nonconstructive*. It purports to prove the existence of a pair of objects with a certain property without supplying an example. It offers two pairs as candidates, but does not tell us which pair actually has the property. To find that out we would have to find out whether or not $\sqrt{2}^{\sqrt{2}}$ is rational. (For the curious, it has turned out to be irrational, but the proof is difficult.) The nonconstructivity of the existence proof derives from its application of the law of the *excluded middle*, $A \lor \neg A$.

Intuitionism was a movement for the revision of classical mathematics that would reject nonconstructive existence proofs and (therefore) the law of the excluded middle. The movement was founded by the Dutch topologist L.E.J. Brouwer in the first decade of the last century, intensely debated in the 1920s, rejected by the vast majority of mathematicians, but continued in Brouwer's version by a small number of disciples, mainly in the Netherlands, and in variant versions by a small number of others around the world, among whom Per Martin-Löf is the acknowledged leader. In the 1970s it was rejuvenated as a movement in philosophy, if not in mathematics, by Michael Dummett.

6.2 THE MEANING OF THE LOGICAL OPERATORS

It is difficult to indicate the motivation for the intuitionist variety of philosophical logic without digressing at least briefly into philosophy of logic and of language. One of the most difficult questions there is that of the meanings of the logical operators. Should we think of the meaning of disjunction, for instance, as deriving from *truth-conditions*, on the order of the following?

(1) "A or B" is true iff A is true or B is true.

Or should we think of it as deriving from *rules of inference*, on the order of the following?

(2) (a) "A or B" may be inferred from A
     (b) "A or B" may be inferred from B
     (c) whatever may be inferred from A and from B
          may be inferred from "A or B"

Even those who agree that (1) and (2) are both acceptable may disagree over which of the two is the more fundamental and which derivative (or whether the meaning of disjunction derives from something different from both).

There are also serious difficulties in regarding either as telling the *whole* story about the meaning of a logical operator. With (1) there is the obvious problem of circularity ("or" appears on both sides of "iff"). With (2) there is the problem that disjunctions are used as premises and conclusions of arguments in many ways other than those indicated in (a)–(c).

Dummett—modernizing Brouwer—maintains that the theory that the grasp of the meaning of disjunction consists in the grasp of truth-conditions (1) cannot account for classical mathematical practice. For whereas classical mathematicians routinely assert disjunctions of the type "$\sqrt{2}^{\sqrt{2}}$ is either rational or irrational" while having no method to verify either disjunct, no sense (it is argued) can be made of the notion of *grasping truth-conditions* for which we have no method of verification.

Dummett holds—again modernizing Brouwer—that what actually guides usage in classical mathematics is simply adherence to certain rules such as those in (2), permitting certain inferential moves; but without truth-conditions connecting these moves to reality, mathematics in its classical form will (it is argued) consist of little more than moves in a game, without any real content. The only mathematics with real content would be a mathematics that goes back to something like (1) while insisting on understanding "truth" as verifiability, even if that requires ceasing to assert many disjunctions formerly asserted.

Brouwer's original intuitionism drew partly on German, partly on Indian sources, and was motivated by idealist philosophy and religious mysticism. Dummett's neo-intuitionism takes inspiration from Wittgenstein, and is motivated by what is unmistakably a form of behaviorism (though that label is deprecated by Dummettians). Thus it is from very different premises that the two are led to the conclusion that "there are no unexperienced truths" (Brouwer) or that "there is no verification-transcendent truth" (Dummett) that was behind the case against classical mathematics just baldly summarized. It would be far beyond the scope of this book to attempt to settle the status of (or even give a full statement of) the very general "idealist" or "anti-realist" claims in metaphysics and theology (Brouwer) or philosophy of language (Dummett) on which the intuitionist or neo-intuitionist case against classical mathematics and its logic is based.

A more modest task is that of attempting to settle what logic would be appropriate *if* the verification-conditional theory of the meaning of the logical operators were accepted; but even this task is really only feasible insofar as it concerns mathematics. The Brouwerian and Dummettian doctrines are of very general scope, but it is only in the case of mathematics that one can see at all clearly the alternative to classical logic to which they lead.

Outside mathematics one would have to contend with the fact that one generally has, by way of verification, not conclusive proof, but only defeasible presumption, which is *nonmonotonic* in the sense that what one is warranted in presuming and asserting given certain information may become unwarranted given more. (Even what is "proved beyond a reasonable doubt" in a criminal case may turn out to be wrong when surprising new evidence is uncovered, whereas what is *mathematically* proved stays proved.) One would also have to contend with the phenomenon of *interference*, with the fact that

performing the operations necessary to verify (or falsify) one assertion may preclude performing the operations necessary to verify (or
falsify) another, a phenomenon conspicuous in but by no means limited to the *quantum* domain. (A DNA sample that could be used to
test either of two hypotheses may be wholly used up testing one of
them, precluding a test of the other; by contrast, operations on numbers to test *mathematical* conjectures always leave the numbers still
available, unchanged, for further operations in test of other conjectures.) The ultimate logic would presumably have to combine formal
features of what in the literature are quite separate nonclassical logics
(nonmonotonic, quantum, and intuitionistic).

6.3 Intuitionistic Sentential Logic

So let us restrict our attention to the logic of mathematical intuitionism. We may start from the following specifications of what
is required for a verification of various logical compounds, more
or less along lines offered by Brouwer's disciples:

(3) A verification of $A \land B$ consists of
     a verification of A and a verification of B.
(4) A verification of $A \lor B$ consists of
     a specification of one of A or B and a verification of it.
(5) A verification of $\neg A$ consists of
     a proof that there cannot be a verification of A.
(6) A verification of $A \to B$ consists of
     the specification of a method and a proof that it
     converts verifications of A into verifications of B.

At first sight, these specifications would seem to leave no room
for inference even by modus ponens. For having a verification of
$A \to B$, which is to say a method of converting A-verifications
into B-verifications, and having also a verification of A, one would
have a method and an input that, if the method were applied to
it, would yield as output the desired verification of B; but one still
would not actually have such a verification. (Having a match and
fuel that, if the match were applied to it, would produce a fire, is
124   still not actually having a fire.)

Dummett accordingly explains—in what is acknowledged even by his critics to be an important clarification—that conditions like (3)–(6) should be thought of as pertaining to *direct* verifications, while the requirement on a *proof* or *demonstration* of A is that to be admissible it must provide at least an *indirect* verification of A, in the sense of a method and a proof that the method would in principle in a finite amount of time produce a direct verification that A. Such indirect verification is sufficient to warrant assertion, and in practice was always so treated by Brouwer.

Thus the familiar sieve of Eratosthenes provides a method that provably would in principle in a finite amount of time produce a direct verification either that 104,729 is prime or that it is composite, and therewith a direct verification of "104,729 is either prime or composite." So a presentation of the sieve method provides an indirect verification of that disjunction, even before we actually apply the sieve method to test 104,729 for primality, and even if we never do apply it. And in practice Brouwer always was willing to assert such a disjunction.

With this understanding, the conditional clause (6) is just what is needed to guarantee that if we have an admissible demonstration of $A \rightarrow B$ and an admissible demonstration of A, then modus ponens provides an admissible demonstration of B. Axiomatizations of intuitionistic sentential logic **I** generally take MP as their only rule.

With the *Heyting axiomatization* we have in addition all formulas of the following forms as axioms:

(7) $A \rightarrow (B \rightarrow A)$
(8) $(A \rightarrow (B \rightarrow C)) \rightarrow ((A \rightarrow B) \rightarrow (A \rightarrow C))$
(9) $(A \rightarrow B) \rightarrow ((A \rightarrow \neg B) \rightarrow \neg A)$
(10) $\neg A \rightarrow (A \rightarrow B)$
(11) $(A \wedge B) \rightarrow A$
(12) $(A \wedge B) \rightarrow B$
(13) $A \rightarrow (B \rightarrow (A \wedge B))$
(14) $A \rightarrow (A \vee B)$
(15) $B \rightarrow (A \vee B)$
(16) $(A \rightarrow C) \rightarrow ((B \rightarrow C) \rightarrow ((A \vee B) \rightarrow C))$

Each of these axioms can be verified, given the understandings (3)–(6), and **I** is therefore sound for its intended interpretation. For

instance, to verify (7) we must produce a method that will convert
an A-verification v into a $(B \to A)$-verification, which is to say, into
a method for converting any B-verification w into an A-verification.
Here is the method: given w, throw it away and replace it by v.

(8) and (9) involve similar ideas, and are left to the reader.

To verify (10), we must produce a method that will convert any
$\neg A$-verification v into a method for converting any A-verification
w into a B-verification. Here is such a method: given v, there can
be no such w, so don't worry, be happy, because any method at
all counts "vacuously" as a method for converting A-verifications
into B-verifications.

(11)–(15) are very easy.

To verify (16) we must produce a method that will convert an
$(A \to C)$-verification u into a method for converting a $(B \to C)$-
verification v into a method for converting an $(A \vee B)$-verification
w into a C-verification. Here is the method: Given w, it is either an
A-verification or a B-verification; in the former case apply u to it
and in the latter case v, to get a C-verification.

We turn next from axioms to theorems. We have already in
section 5.8, using just (7) and (8), obtained the deduction theorem and several theorems:

(17) $A \to A$
(18) $(A \to (B \to C)) \to (B \to (A \to C))$
(19) $(A \to B) \to ((B \to C) \to (A \to C))$

Two significant theorems are the following laws of double negation and contraposition:

(20) $A \to \neg\neg A$
(21) $(A \to B) \to (\neg B \to \neg A)$

Proof of (20).

i	A	Hyp	i
ii	$(\neg A \to (A \to \neg\neg A)) \to$ $(A \to (\neg A \to \neg\neg A))$	18	
iii	$\neg A \to (A \to \neg\neg A)$	Ax	
iv	$A \to (\neg A \to \neg\neg A)$	ii, iii, MP	
v	$\neg A \to \neg\neg A$	i, iv, MP	i
vi	$\neg A \to \neg A$	17	

vii	$(\neg A \to \neg A) \to$		
	$((\neg A \to \neg\neg A) \to \neg\neg A)$	Ax	
viii	$(\neg A \to \neg\neg A) \to \neg\neg A$	vi, vii, MP	
ix	$\neg\neg A$	v, viii, MP	i

(20) then follows from i and ix by Ded.

Proof of (21).

i	$A \to B$	Hyp	i
ii	$\neg B$	Hyp	ii
iii	$\neg B \to (A \to \neg B)$	Ax	
iv	$A \to \neg B$	ii, iii	ii
v	$(A \to \neg B) \to \neg A$	9, i, MP	i
vi	$\neg A$	iv, v, MP	i, ii
vii	$\neg B \to \neg A$	ii, vi, Ded	i

(21) then follows from i and vii by Ded.

Now (21) and its substitution instance $(\neg B \to \neg A) \to (\neg\neg A \to \neg\neg B)$ with (19) yield the following:

(21') $(A \to B) \to (\neg\neg A \to \neg\neg B)$

Here are a very similar item and an easy corollary (wherein the biconditional abbreviates as always the conjunction of a conditional and its converse), whose proofs are left to the reader:

(22) $(A \to \neg B) \to (B \to \neg A)$
(23) $\neg\neg\neg A \leftrightarrow \neg A$

6.4 Double-Negation Interpretation

Conspicuously missing from the list of theorems is the converse of (20) and excluded middle:

(24) $\neg\neg A \to A$
(25) $A \lor \neg A$

Add either as an axiom and the other becomes a theorem.

Proofs. In one direction, in **I** (14) and (15) and (21) together give $\neg(A \lor \neg A) \to \neg A$ and $\neg(A \lor \neg A) \to \neg\neg A$, and then

(9) gives $\neg\neg(A \vee \neg A)$. So if we had (24) we would have (25). In the other direction (7) gives $A \to (\neg\neg A \to A)$ while (10) with (18) give $\neg A \to (\neg\neg A \to A)$, and then (16) gives $(A \vee \neg A) \to (\neg\neg A \to A)$, which is to say, $(25) \to (24)$.

In fact adding either (24) or (25) to **I** gives what is known to be a complete axiomatization of classical sentential logic (though the proof will be deferred). Returning to what can be proved in **I** without further axioms, here is another key theorem:

(26) $\neg\neg(\neg\neg A \to A)$

Proof.

i	$(A \to (\neg\neg A \to A)) \to (\neg(\neg\neg A \to A) \to \neg A)$	22
ii	$A \to (\neg\neg A \to A)$	7
iii	$\neg(\neg\neg A \to A) \to \neg A$	i, ii, MP
iv	$(\neg\neg\neg A \to (\neg\neg A \to A)) \to$ $(\neg(\neg\neg A \to A) \to \neg\neg\neg\neg A)$	21
v	$\neg\neg\neg A \to (\neg\neg A \to A)$	10
vi	$\neg(\neg\neg A \to A) \to \neg\neg\neg\neg A$	iv, v, MP
vii	$\neg\neg\neg\neg A \to \neg\neg A$	23
viii	$(\neg(\neg\neg A \to A) \to \neg\neg\neg\neg A) \to$ $((\neg\neg\neg\neg A \to \neg\neg A) \to (\neg(\neg\neg A \to A) \to \neg\neg A))$	19
ix	$(\neg\neg\neg\neg A \to \neg\neg A) \to$ $(\neg(\neg\neg A \to A) \to \neg\neg A)$	vi, viii, MP
x	$\neg(\neg\neg A \to A) \to \neg\neg A$	vii, ix, MP
xi	$(\neg(\neg\neg A \to A) \to \neg A)) \to$ $((\neg(\neg\neg A \to A) \to \neg\neg A) \to \neg\neg(\neg\neg A \to A))$	9
xii	$(\neg(\neg\neg A \to A) \to \neg\neg A) \to$ $\neg\neg(\neg\neg A \to A)$	iii, xi, MP

(26) then follows form x and xii by MP.

There is a related item:

(27) $\neg\neg(A \to B) \to (\neg\neg A \to \neg\neg B)$

Proof. We give only a sketch of the proof, noting these main steps along the way:

$(A \to B) \to (A \to B)$

$A \to ((A \to B) \to B)$

$$A \to (\neg B \to \neg(A \to B))$$
$$A \to (\neg\neg(A \to B) \to \neg\neg B)$$
$$\neg\neg(A \to B) \to (A \to \neg\neg B)$$
$$\neg\neg(A \to B) \to (\neg\neg\neg B \to \neg A)$$
$$\neg\neg(A \to B) \to (\neg\neg A \to \neg\neg\neg\neg B)$$

From (20) it follows that the double negation of any of (7)–(16) is a theorem of **I**, and from (26) that the same is true for (24). Moreover, (27) with MP tells us that if $\neg\neg(A \to B)$ and $\neg\neg A$ are theorems of **I**, so is $\neg\neg B$. It follows that if we go through a classical demonstration and double negate every line, each line will become an intuitionistic theorem. Thus *the double negation of any classical theorem is an intuitionistic theorem.*

This fact together with (23) tells us that any classical theorem beginning with $\neg$ is an intuitionistic theorem. Now a classical tautology in which only $\neg$ and $\wedge$ occur must either begin with $\neg$ and so be a theorem of **I**, or be a conjunction of some number of classical tautologies that begin with $\neg$ and so are theorems of **I**. But using (13), any conjunction of theorems of **I** is a theorem of **I**. So *any classical theorem in which only $\neg$ and $\wedge$ occur is an intuitionistic theorem.*

Given any formula A involving $\neg$ and $\wedge$ and $\vee$ and $\to$, we can associate a classically equivalent formula as follows:

(28) $p^* = p$
(29) $(\neg A)^* = \neg A^*$
(30) $(A \wedge B)^* = A^* \wedge B^*$
(31) $(A \vee B)^* = \neg(\neg A^* \wedge \neg B^*)$
(32) $(A \to B)^* = \neg(A^* \wedge \neg B^*)$

In other words, A^* is the result of eliminating $\vee$ and $\to$ using their classical definitions in terms of $\neg$ and $\wedge$. Then *for any classical theorem A, the translation A^* is an intuitionistic theorem.*

And thus while from one point of view intuitionistic logic is a part of classical logic, missing one axiom, from another point of view classical logic is a part of intuitionistic logic, missing two connectives, intuitionistic $\vee$ and $\to$ (which are *not* intuitionistically equivalent to any compound involving just $\neg$ and $\wedge$). From this latter point of view, what the classical logician accepts in accepting

$A \vee \neg A$ or $\neg\neg A \to A$ is not what the intuitionist rejects in rejecting these same formulas. For the translations of $A \vee \neg A$ and $\neg\neg A \to A$ are just $\neg(\neg A \wedge \neg\neg A)$ and $\neg(\neg\neg A \wedge \neg A)$, both of which are perfectly acceptable intuitionistically.

6.5 THE MODAL INTERPRETATION

Every intuitionistic assertion is supposed to require a verification or "constructive proof." This fact suggested to Gödel the possibility of interpreting **I** in a modal logic appropriate to some notion $\Box$ of constructive provability or demonstrability, in such a way that every intuitionistic formula A is translated as a modal formula $A^\dagger$ that is (or is equivalent to) one beginning with $\Box$. As we saw in section 3.8, the leading candidate for a logic of demonstrability is **S4**, and it was an interpretation in **S4** that Gödel proposed. The fact that in **S4** $\Box(\Box A \wedge \Box B)$ is provably equivalent to $(\Box A \wedge \Box B)$, and similarly for $\vee$, allows for slight variations in the translation.

The simplest translation is the following:

(33) $p^\dagger \quad\quad = \Box p$
(34) $(A \wedge B)^\dagger \quad = A^\dagger \wedge B^\dagger$
(35) $(A \vee B)^\dagger \quad = A^\dagger \vee B^\dagger$
(36) $(A \to B)^\dagger \quad = \Box(A^\dagger \to B^\dagger)$
(37) $(\neg A)^\dagger \quad = \Box\neg A^\dagger$

Gödel announced the following result without proof:

(38) A is a theorem of **I** iff $A^\dagger$ is a theorem of **S4**

This result together with the (historically later) result that **S4** is decidable implies that **I** is decidable. Of course, given the Gödel translation, the intuitionistic rejection of $p \vee \neg p$ becomes unremarkable, since its translation is $\Box p \vee \Box\neg\Box p$, which though a theorem of **S5** is not a theorem of **S4**.

The proof of Gödel's illuminating result is much facilitated by the later machinery of Kripke models. A Kripke model $U = (U, \prec, V)$ for **I** will be a reflexive, transitive frame (as for **S4**) together with a valuation that is *hereditary*, in the sense that if V makes p

true at u and $u \prec v$, then V makes p true at v. The definition of truth runs as follows:

(39) $\quad U \vDash p_i[u]$ $\qquad$ iff $\quad V(i, u) = 1$

(40) $\quad U \vDash (A \wedge B)[u]$ $\quad$ iff $\quad U \vDash A[u]$ and $U \vDash B[u]$

(41) $\quad U \vDash (A \vee B)[u]$ $\quad$ iff $\quad U \vDash A[u]$ or $U \vDash B[u]$

(42) $\quad U \vDash \neg A[u]$ $\qquad$ iff $\quad$ for all v with $u \prec v$, not $U \vDash A[v]$

(43) $\quad U \vDash (A \rightarrow B)[u]$ $\quad$ iff $\quad$ for all v with $u \prec v$, if $U \vDash A[v]$, $U \vDash B[v]$

It is not hard to show by induction on complexity that we have:

(44) $\quad$ if $U \vDash A[u]$ and $u \prec v$, then $U \vDash A[v]$

Proof. Indeed, (44) holds for atomic A by the hereditary requirement on V. If (44) holds for A and for B, then it holds for their conjunction, since if $U \vDash (A \wedge B)[u]$, then $U \vDash A[u]$ and $U \vDash B[u]$ by one direction of (40), hence if $u \prec v$, then $U \vDash A[v]$ and $U \vDash B[v]$ by (44) for A and for B, and so $U \vDash (A \wedge B)[v]$ by the other direction of (40). The case of $\vee$ is similar. If (44) holds for A, then it holds for $\neg A$, since if $U \vDash \neg A[u]$, then if $u \prec w$, then not $U \vDash A[w]$ by one direction of (42), so in particular if $u \prec v$, then if $v \prec w$ not $U \vDash A[w]$, since transitivity implies $u \prec w$, and this shows $U \vDash \neg A[v]$ by the other direction of (42). The case of $\rightarrow$ is similar.

An arbitrary Kripke model $(U, \prec, W)$ for **S4** gives rise to a Kripke model $(U, \prec, V)$ for **I** where V makes p true at u iff W makes $\Box p$ true at u. (So if W was already hereditary, $V = W$.) Comparing (33)–(37) with (39)–(43) and with the clauses in the definition of truth in a Kripke model for modal logic, it can be seen that we have

(45) $\quad (U, \prec, V) \vDash A[u]$ $\qquad$ iff $\quad (U, \prec, W) \vDash A^\dagger[u]$

Gödel's result (38) follows as soon as we have established the soundness and completeness of **I** for the Kripke model theory just set up. For soundness the proof is, as usual, tedious but routine.

Proof. For (7) we must show that for any u, for any v with $u \prec v$ we have that if $U \vDash A[v]$, then $U \vDash (B \rightarrow A)[u']$, which is to say that for any w with $v \prec w$ we have that if $U \vDash B[w]$, then $U \vDash A[w]$. And indeed, whether or not $U \vDash B[w]$, we have $U \vDash A[w]$ if $u \prec v \prec w$ by transitivity, which gives $u \prec w$, together with the hereditary property (44). For (8) the proof is similar, and is left to the reader; indeed, the cases of all the other axioms are similar.

Soundness already by itself, without yet having completeness, enables us to use Kripke models to show that the laws of excluded middle $p \vee \neg p$ and double negation $\neg\neg p \rightarrow p$ and $\neg p \vee \neg\neg p$ are *not* theorems of **I**.

Proof. Indeed, in a reflexive and transitive Kripke model with just two states, $u \prec v$, with p true only at v, we see p fails at u, but also $\neg p$ fails at u (because p holds at v and $u \prec v$), and so $p \vee \neg p$ fails at u and is not a theorem of **I**; likewise $\neg\neg p \rightarrow p$ fails, since $\neg\neg p$ holds at u. In a reflexive and transitive Kripke model with three states with $u \prec v$ and $u \prec v'$ and p true only at v, $\neg p \vee \neg\neg p$ fails at u, because $\neg p$ and $\neg\neg p$ both fail, there being on the one hand a v with $u \prec v$ and p true at v and on the other hand a v' with $u \prec v'$ and $\neg p$ true at v'.

The proof of completeness will be put in a separate section.

6.6 COMPLETENESS IN THE TECHNICAL SENSE

For completeness the proof is an adaptation of the method used for modal logic in section 3.6 (which the reader may do well to review before proceeding further). Define a formula B to be *deducible* from a set t of formulas iff there is a deduction from hypotheses with premises in t and conclusion B. Call u *deductively closed* iff every B deducible from u is already in u. Let the *deductive closure* t^* of t be the set of all B deducible from t. It is easy to see (stringing together deductions) that a conclusion deducible from intermediate steps deducible from premises in t is deducible from those same premises, and (hence) that the deductive closure of a set t is deductively closed, as the terminology would suggest.

Call t *bisective* iff whenever a disjunction $A \vee B$ is in t, either A is in t or B is in t. Call t *negation inconsistent* iff for some B

both it and its negation $\neg B$ are deducible from t and *absolutely inconsistent* iff every formula is deducible from t. The presence of axiom (10) guarantees that negation inconsistency implies absolute inconsistency. Since the converse is trivial we may use "consistent" unambiguously. The properties of deductive closure, bisectiveness, and consistency may be likened to courage (of its convictions), justice, and temperance, and a set with all three called *virtuous*. We have the following analogue of Lindenbaum's lemma:

(46) If t is a consistent set of formulas, then t is a subset of u for some virtuous set of formulas u.

Proof. We enumerate all disjunctions $A_0 \vee B_0, A_1 \vee B_1$, and so on, let C be any formula not deducible from t (there must be one by consistency), and let t_0 be the deductive closure of t. Having t_n, deductively closed and not containing C, if C is deducible from t_n together with $A_n \vee B_n$, let $t_{n+1} = t_n$. Otherwise, either (i) C is not deducible from t_n together with A_n or (ii) C is not deducible from t_n together with B_n. For otherwise by the deduction theorem $A_n \to C$ and $B_n \to C$ would be deducible from t_n, and the presence of axiom (16) would guarantee that $(A_n \vee B_n) \to C$ is deducible from t_n, and C from t_n plus $A_n \vee B_n$, contrary to assumption. In case (i) (respectively, (ii)) let t_{n+1} be the deductive closure of t_n plus A_n (respectively, B_n). Let u be the union of the t_n. Since any deduction from u uses only finitely many premises from u and these all belong to t_n for some n, and since each t_n is deductively closed and does not contain C, u is deductively closed and does not contain C (and hence is consistent). Moreover, if neither disjunct of a disjunction $A_n \vee B_n$ belongs to u, it is because C (which is not deducible from u) was deducible from the disjunction together with the subset t_n of u, which implies that the disjunction is not in u. Hence u is bisective, to complete the proof.

We also have the following key lemmas:

(47) (a) If t is virtuous, then $A \wedge B$ is in t iff A is in t and B is in t.

(b) If t is virtuous, then $A \lor B$ is in t iff A is in t or B is in t.

Proof. For (47), the (a) part uses (deductive closure and) axioms (11) and (12) in the "only if" direction, and (13) in the "if" direction, while the (b) part uses axioms (14) and (15) in the "if" direction and bisectiveness in the "only if" direction.

(48) (a) If t is virtuous and $\neg A$ is not in t,
then there is a virtuous u containing t and A.

(b) If t is virtuous and $A \to B$ is not in t,
then there is a virtuous u containing t and A but not B.

Proof. For the (b) part, since $A \to B$ is not deducible from t, by the deduction theorem B is not deducible from t together with A. The proof of (46) (with B in the role of C) produces the required u. The (a) part is similar. Note in connection with (48) that trivially, (a) if $\neg A$ *is* in t, then no consistent and hence no virtuous u can contain both t and A; and (b), if $A \to B$ is in t, then no deductively closed and hence no virtuous u can contain t and A without containing B.

Now let the *canonical Kripke model* $\mathbf{U} = (U, \subseteq, V)$ be defined as follows. U is the set of all virtuous sets, $\subseteq$ is the usual set-theoretic inclusion relation, and V makes p true at u iff p is in u. One proves that for all u in U and all formulas A we have the following:

(49) $\mathbf{U} \vDash A[u]$ iff $A \in u$

The proof is by induction on complexity.

Proof. The atomic case is true by definition of V, and the conjunction, disjunction, negation, and conditional cases are proved by comparing the clauses (40), (41), (42), (43) in the definition of truth in a Kripke model with lemmas (47a), (47b), (48a), (48b), respectively.

In particular, if C is not demonstrable, the proof of (46) (taking t as the empty set) establishes the existence of a virtuous u not containing C, and (45) then implies that C is not true at this u in the canonical Kripke model, and therefore not valid, proving completeness (and with it Gödel's result and the decidability of **I**).

Digression. Note that if we added (24) or equivalently (25) as an axiom, deductive closure would imply that (25) is in any virtuous set, and bisectiveness would then imply that for any virtuous set u and any formula A, either A is in u or $\neg A$ is in u. Then defining a classical valuation on sentence letters p by letting V make p true iff p is in u, it would be easy to prove along lines similar to the foregoing that for any formula A, V makes A true iff A is in u. If A is not a theorem of the logic, the proof of (46) (with A in the role of B) shows that there is a virtuous u with A not in u, and so we have a classical valuation V that does not make A true, and A is not a tautology. This suffices to prove what was asserted in passing earlier, that **I** plus (24) or (25) is complete for classical sentential logic.

6.7 INTERMEDIATE LOGICS

There are a couple of logics of intermediate between **I** and classical sentential logic that are often mentioned in the literature, and that like **I** itself turn out to have interesting connections with modal logics. **KC** and **LC** are, respectively, the results of adding to **I** the following axioms:

(50) $\neg A \vee \neg\neg A$
(51) $(A \to B) \vee (B \to A)$

(50) is valid for R-convergent (reflexive, transitive) frames. For in order for (50) to fail at u, each disjunct must fail, and so there must be a v with $u \prec v$ where A is true and a v' with $u \prec v'$ where $\neg A$ is true. Then for any w with $v \prec w$, A is true at w by heredity, and for any w with $v' \prec w$, A is not true at w by the negation clause in the definition of truth in a Kripke model. So there can be no w with $v \prec w$ and $v' \prec w$, and R-convergence fails.

(51) is valid for R-total (reflexive, transitive) frames. For in order for (51) to fail at u, each disjunct must fail, and so there must be a v with $u \prec v$ where A holds and B fails, and a v' with $u \prec v'$ where B holds and A fails. But then by heredity, A holds at any

135

w with $v \prec w$ and B holds at any w with $v' \prec w$, so we can have neither $v \prec v'$ nor $v' \prec v$, and R-totality fails.

A reflexive, transitive frame where (50) fails has already been described, showing that (50) is not a theorem of **I**. We leave it to the reader to find a reflexive, transitive, R-convergent frame where (51) fails, showing that (51) is not a theorem of **KC**. We also leave it to the reader to show that, by contrast, (50) *is* a theorem of **LC**. (It will be useful to prove first that

$$(A \rightarrow \neg A) \rightarrow \neg A$$
$$(\neg A \rightarrow A) \rightarrow \neg\neg A$$

are theorems of **I**.)

This last result follows indirectly from the following extensions of Gödel's result (38):

(52) A is a theorem of **KC** iff $A^\dagger$ is a theorem of **S4.2**.
(53) A is a theorem of **LC** iff $A^\dagger$ is a theorem of **S4.3**.

These in turn follow from the pertinent completeness results. **KC** is complete for R-convergent, transitive, reflexive frames. **LC** is complete for R-total, transitive, reflexive frames.

> *Proofs.* For **KC**, it is enough to show that if u, v, v' are virtuous and $u \subseteq v \cap v'$, there is a virtuous w such that $v \cup v' \subseteq w$. For the existence of such a w it is enough that $v \cup v'$ be consistent, that there is no A in v with $\neg A$ in v' or vice versa. But since u is deductively closed, it contains each instance of axiom (50), and since it is bisective, for each A either $\neg A$ is in u or $\neg\neg A$ is in u, and so either there can be no v with $u \subseteq v$ and A in v or there can be no v' with $u \subseteq v'$ and $\neg A$ in v'. For **LC**, it is enough to show that if u, v, w are virtuous and $u \subseteq v \cap w$, then either $v \subseteq w$ or $w \subseteq v$. We leave the task of doing so to the reader.

6.8 Intuitionistic Predicate Logic

The analogues of (3) and (4) are these, where "any" and "some" are tacitly understood as restricted to a certain pertinent universe of objects:

(54) A verification of $\forall xA$ consists of
a method and a proof that applying it to any u produces
a verification that A holds for u

(55) A verification of $\exists xA$ consists of
the production of some u and
the verification that A holds for u.

The rule of universal generalization and the following axioms turn out to be intuitively sound for intuitionistic as for classical logic:

(56) $\forall xA \rightarrow A(y/x)$ y free for x in A
(57) $A(y/x) \rightarrow \exists xA$ y free for x in A
(58) $\forall x(A \rightarrow B) \rightarrow (A \rightarrow \forall xB)$ x not free in A
(59) $\forall x(A \rightarrow B) \rightarrow (\exists xA \rightarrow B)$ x not free in B

The double negation interpretation can be extended to intuitionistic predicate logic with these axioms and rules, and the modal interpretation can be extended to an interpretation in a quantified modal logic obtained by combining classical predicate logic with these axioms and rules with the sentential modal logic **S4** (with the result that the converse Barcan formula becomes demonstrable).

The notion of Kripke model can be extended as well. Such a model will have (i) a set T, (ii) a relation $\prec$, (iii) for each t in T a set U_t, the universe of objects existing at t, subject to the requirement that if $t \prec t'$, then $U_t \subseteq U_{t'}$, and (v) a specification for each one-place predicate letter P and each t in T and each u in U_t whether or not P is true of u at t, subject to the requirement that $t \prec t'$ and u is in U_t and P is true of u at t, then P is true of u at t', and similarly for many-place predicates. Soundness and completeness hold. Considerations of space preclude presentation of this whole body of material here.

A few facts may be just mentioned as an indication of the complexity of intuitionistic predicate logic. Thus in place of the classical four:

(60) *universal affirmative:* $\forall \equiv \neg\exists\neg$
(61) *particular affirmative:* $\exists \equiv \neg\forall\neg$
(62) *universal negative:* $\neg\exists \equiv \forall\neg$
(63) *particular negative:* $\neg\forall \equiv \exists\neg$

we have ten, in which under a single number (a) implies (b) and (b) implies (c):

(60') (a) $\forall$
       (b) $\neg\neg\forall$
       (c) $\forall\neg\neg \equiv \neg\neg\forall\neg\neg \equiv \neg\exists\neg$
(61') (a) $\exists$
       (b) $\exists\neg\neg$
       (c) $\neg\neg\exists \equiv \neg\neg\exists\neg\neg \equiv \neg\forall\neg$
(62') $\neg\exists \equiv \forall\neg \equiv \neg\exists\neg\neg \equiv \neg\neg\forall\neg$
(63') (a) $\exists\neg$
       (b) $\neg\neg\exists\neg \equiv \neg\forall\neg\neg$
       (c) $\neg\forall$

Kripke models can be used to show that the implications do not reverse. For instance, in a Kripke model with just two states $t_0 \prec t_1$ and the same universe $\{0\}$ at both, with P untrue of 0 at t_0 but true at t_1, we see that $\neg\neg\forall xPx$ holds but $\forall xPx$ fails at t_0. In a Kripke model with infinitely many states $t_0 \prec t_1 \prec t_2 \prec \ldots$ and with the universe of t_n being $\{0, 1, \ldots, n\}$ and P being true at t_n of every element of the universe but n, we see that $\forall x\neg\neg Px$ holds but $\neg\neg\forall xPx$ fails at t_0.

The fact that it was necessary to use an infinite model in the second example is significant. This is never necessary in classical monadic or one-place predicate logic, and this fact is at the root of the proof that classical monadic predicate logic is decidable. By contrast, intuitionistic monadic predicate logic turns out to be undecidable.

6.9 COMPLETENESS IN THE INTUITIVE SENSE

Though Kripke models are certainly useful, they are *not* a "semantics" in any serious, linguistic sense, and their connection to the intended meaning of the intuitionist logical operators as explained in (3)–(6) and (50)–(51) is obscure. The question whether even intuitionistic sentential logic is complete for its *intended* interpretation—the question whether every sentential logical formula all of whose instances, obtained by substituting sentences of intuitionistic mathematics for the sentence letters, are intuition-istically correct is a theorem of **I**—is *not* settled by the proof of completeness for the *technical* interpretation provided by Kripke models. Indeed, the question of correctness for the intended interpretation cannot be settled without deep involvement in intuitionistic mathematics, just as the question of what is the correct temporal logic for special or general relativity cannot be settled without deep involvement in relativistic physics.

The central notion in intuitionistic mathematics is that of the *infinitely proceeding* or *potentially infinite* sequence of natural numbers. (This part of Brouwerianism is retained by hard-core Dutch intuitionists but abandoned by the Martin-Löf school.) In Brouwer's mentalistic or psychologistic version, such a sequence is generated by successive choices of "the creative mathematical subject."

The subject may choose at any point to impose limitations on his—the masculine pronoun is used because the subject in question in Brouwer's account is none other than Brouwer himself—future freedom of choice, say requiring that henceforth only even numbers are to be chosen. In the extreme case, the creative mathematical subject may choose to abolish all freedom from the beginning and lay down at the outset a definite law dictating what all terms of the sequence are to be. This extreme case gives the notion of a *lawlike* sequence.

The subject may also choose—at least according to one interpretation of a more than usually cryptic discussion of Brouwer's—at any point to impose restrictions on his future freedom to impose restrictions on his future freedom. In the extreme case, the creative mathematical subject may choose to abolish all freedom to restrict freedom from the beginning and lay down at the outset a definite law dictating that each term of the sequence must result from an independent act of free choice. This extreme case gives the notion of a *lawless* sequence.

The subject may also choose—it seems—at any point to impose restrictions on his future freedom to impose restrictions on his future freedom to impose restrictions on his future freedom. In the extreme case, the creative mathematical subject may choose to abolish all freedom to restrict freedom to restrict freedom from the beginning and lay down at the outset a definite law dictating that terms are to be chosen freely except insofar as restrictions on freedom have been chosen freely. The bulk of Brouwer's writings on infinitely proceeding sequences in fact pertains to this case: freedom and freedom to restrict freedom, without higher-order restrictions.

It is easily seen intuitively that, letting α be a variable ranging over lawless sequences, and writing $\alpha(n)$ for the nth term of α, we have:

$$(64) \quad \neg\exists\alpha\forall n\, \alpha(n) = 0$$

or equivalently:

$$(65) \quad \forall\alpha\neg\exists n\, \alpha(n) \neq 0$$

(The equivalence of (64) and (65) holds even intuitionistically.) For intuitionistically, $\forall n\, \alpha(n) = 0$ requires a *proof*, and at the time any proof was produced, only finitely many terms of α would have been chosen, and the only information available with which to prove anything about α would be the fact that the terms chosen so far are what they are, and that α is lawless. But any supposed proof from *this* information that all future choices will be 0 could be immediately defied and refuted by the creative mathematical subject choosing 1 for the very next term. More subtle and sophisticated considerations are supposed to show that equally we have

$$(66) \quad \neg\forall\alpha\exists n\, \alpha(n) \neq 0$$

Now (65) and (66) already give us $\neg\forall p(p \vee \neg p)$ where p ranges over sentences of intuitionistic mathematics (such as $\exists n\, \alpha(n) \neq 0$). (We cannot hope to get $\exists p\neg(p \vee \neg p)$, since we have the double negation of any classical sentential theorem and in particular $\forall p\neg\neg(p \vee \neg p)$.) In fact assuming an appropriate theory of lawless sequences, it can be shown intuitionistically that if $A(p, q, \ldots)$ is not a theorem of **I**, then there is finite Kripke model in which $A(p, q, \ldots)$ fails, and from that Kripke model we can obtain an intuitionistic proof of the following assertion of invalidity:

$$(67) \quad \neg\forall\alpha\forall\beta\ldots A(\exists n\, \alpha(n) \neq 0, \exists n\, \beta(n) \neq 0, \ldots)$$

140 and hence of $\neg\forall p\forall q\ldots A(p, q, \ldots)$.

But all this is assuming the theory of lawless sequences. Without that theory one can at least give an example of a *lawlike* sequence γ for which we *are not in a position to assert* that $\exists n \, \gamma(n) \neq 0 \vee \neg \exists n \, \gamma(n) \neq 0$. Such a γ is provided by letting $\gamma(n) = 0$ or 1 according as there is not or is a counterexample to Goldbach's conjecture $\leq n$, that is, an even number $4 \leq 2m \leq n$ that cannot be written as a sum $2m = r + s$ of two primes.

Even *with* the theory of lawless sequences the situation is unsatisfactory at the level of monadic predicate rather than sentential logic. Despite vast amounts of work on other intuitionism-related topics, the question of the completeness of the full intuitionistic logic for its intended interpretation is not yet fully resolved.

6.10 FURTHER READING

Brouwer's key texts, "Intuitionism and Formalism" and "Consciousness, Philosophy, and Mathematics," have been multiply anthologized, but for the latter one should be sure to consult the unexpurgated version in Brouwer (1976) rather than the version in Benacerraf & Putnam (1983), which "keeps the Kant but drops the Krishna," retaining allusions to the *Kritik der reinen Vernunft* while suppressing quotations from the *Bhagavad Gita*, leaving an incomplete picture of Brouwer's motivations. Another historical source still widely read is Gödel (1933), where the modal interpretation first appeared. The little book Heyting (1956) is an introduction to intuitionistic mathematics and logic by the Brouwer disciple who first offered a formal presentation of intuitionistic logic, though the treatment of logic in the final chapter there is not extensive. A proof of the completeness of Heyting's intuitionistic sentential logic for its intended interpretation, adapting work of Georg Kreisel on lawless sequences to the context of Kripke models, is presented in Burgess (1981b).

Again as with relevantism the present author has a reputation—based on the polemical Burgess (1984b) and its sequel Burgess (2005b)—for being hostile, if not to intuitionism as such, then anyhow to Dummettian *neo*-intuitionism; so again a second opinion may be especially desirable. Neo-intuitionism was launched by Dummett (1973). Prawitz (1977) is one of the earliest and most important of many commentaries. Nearly everything Dummett has written subsequently is pertinent to "anti-realism," but Dummett (1976) and Dummett (1992) stand out. It may be mentioned that by the time one comes to the book just cited, Dummett's case for intuitionism has come to look rather different from how it looked in the paper of two decades earlier (on which the sketch in section 6.2 was based). The case for intuitionism is again restated in the concluding philosophical remarks in Dummett (2000); the rest of that book is an excellent and evenhanded introduction to intuitionistic mathematics and its logic as a whole. The bulk of the literature on Dummettian "anti-realism," however, belongs distinctly to philosophy of language, while the bulk of the other literature on intuitionism belongs distinctly to mathematical logic.

References

Adams, Ernest
> (1975) *The Logic of Conditionals: An Application of Probability to Deductive Logic*, Synthese Library 86 (Dordrecht: Reidel).

Anderson, Alan Ross, and Nuel D. Belnap, Jr.
> (1975) *Entailment: The Logic of Relevance and Necessity*, vol. 1 (Princeton, NJ: Princeton University Press).

Anderson, Alan Ross, Nuel D. Belnap, Jr., and Michael Dunn
> (1992) *Entailment: The Logic of Relevance and Necessity*, vol. 2 (Princeton, NJ: Princeton University Press).

Benacerraf, Paul, and Hilary Putnam
> (1983) (eds.) *Philosophy of Mathematics: Selected Readings*, 2nd ed. (Cambridge: Cambridge University Press).

Bennett, Jonathan
> (2003) *A Philosophical Guide to Conditionals* (Oxford: Oxford University Press).

Benthem, Johann van
> (1991) *Logic and Time*, 2nd ed., Synthese Library 156 (Dordrecht: Kluwer).

Blackburn, Patrick, Maarten de Rijke, and Yde Venema
> (2002) *Modal Logic* (Cambridge: Cambridge University Press).

Blamey, Stephen
> (1986) "Partial Logic," in (Gabbay & Guenthner, 1986), 1–70.

Boolos, George
> (1993) *The Logic of Provability* (Cambridge: Cambridge University Press).

Brouwer, L.E.J.
> (1976) *Collected Works*, vol. 1: *Philosophy and Foundations of Mathematics*, A. Heyting, ed. (Amsterdam: North Holland).

Bull, Robert A., and Krister Segerberg
> (1984) "Basic Modal Logic," in (Gabbay & Guenthner, 1984), 1–88.

Burgess, John P.
> (1979) "The Unreal Future," *Theoria* (Lund) 44: 157–79.
> (1980) "Decidability for Branching Time," *Studia Logica* 39: 203–18.

References

(1981a) "The Completeness of Intuitionistic Propositional Calculus for Its Intended Interpretation," *Notre Dame Journal of Formal Logic* 22: 17–28.

(1981b) "Quick Completeness Proofs for Some Logics of Conditionals," *Notre Dame Journal of Formal Logic* 22: 76–84.

(1981c) "Relevance: A Fallacy?" *Notre Dame Journal of Formal Logic* 22: 97–104.

(1982a) "Axioms for Tense Logic, I. Since & Until," *Notre Dame Journal of Formal Logic* 23: 367–74.

(1982b) "Axioms for Tense Logic, II. Time Periods," *Notre Dame Journal of Formal Logic* 23: 375–83.

(1983) "Common Sense and 'Relevance,'" *Notre Dame Journal of Formal Logic* 24: 41–53.

(1984a) "Basic Tense Logic," in (Gabbay & Guenthner, 1984), 98–134.

(1984b) "Dummett's Case for Intuitionism," *History and Philosophy of Logic* 5, 177–94.

(1992) "Proofs about Proofs: A Defense of Classical Logic," in M. Detlefsen, ed., *Proof, Logic and Formalization* (London: Routledge), 8–23.

(1998) "*Quinus ab Omne Nævo Vindicatus*," in A. A. Kazmi, ed., *Meaning and Reference, Canadian Journal of Philosophy Supplement* 23: 25–65.

(1999) "Which Modal Logic Is the Right One?," *Notre Dame Journal of Formal Logic* 40: 81–93.

(2003) "Which Modal Models Are the Right Ones (for Logical Necessity)?," *Theoria* (San Sebastian) 18: 145–58.

(2005a) "No Requirement of Relevance," in (Shapiro, 2005), 727–50.

(2005b) "On Anti-Anti-Realism," *Facta Philosophica* 7: 121–44.

Burgess, John P., and Yuri Gurevich

(1985) "The Decision Problem for Linear Temporal Logic," *Notre Dame Journal of Formal Logic* 26, 115–28.

Carnap, Rudolf

(1946) "Modalities and Quantification," *Journal of Symbolic Logic* 11: 33–64.

Comrie, Bernard

(1976) *Aspect* (Cambridge: Cambridge Textbooks in Linguistics, Cambridge University Press).

(1985) *Tense* (Cambridge: Cambridge Textbooks in Linguistics, Cambridge University Press).

Cresswell, Max

(1990) *Entities and Indices* (Dordrecht: Kluwer).

Dummett, Michael

(1973) "The Philosophical Basis of Intuitionistic Logic," in H. E. Rose and J. C. Sheperdson, eds., *Logical Colloquium '73* (Amsterdam: North Holland), reprinted in (Dummett, 1978) and (Benacerraf & Putnam, 1983).

(1976) "The Justification of Deduction," *Mind* 85: 112–19, reprinted in (Dummett, 1978).

(1978) *Truth and Other Enigmas* (Cambridge, MA: Harvard University Press).

(1992) *The Logical Basis of Metaphysics* (Cambridge, MA: Harvard University Press).

(2000) *Elements of Intuitionism* (Oxford: Oxford University Press).

Edgington, Dorothy

(2001) "Conditionals," in (Goble, 2001), 385–414.

Epstein, Richard

(1996) *The Semantic Foundations of Logic: Propositional Logic* (Belmont, CA: Wadsworth).

Gabbay, Dov M., and Franz Guenthner

(1983) (eds.) *Handbook of Philosophical Logic*, vol. 1: *Classical Logic* (Dordrecht: Reidel).

(1984) (eds.) *Handbook of Philosophical Logic*, vol. 2: *Extensions of Classical Logic* (Dordrecht: Reidel).

(1986) (eds.) *Handbook of Philosophical Logic*, vol. 3: *Alternatives to Classical Logic* (Dordrecht: Reidel).

(1989) (eds.) *Handbook of Philosophical Logic*, vol. 4: *Topics in Philosophy of Language* (Dordrecht: Reidel).

Garson, James

(1984) "Quantification in Modal Logic," in (Gabbay & Guenthner, 1984), 249–308.

Goble, Lou

(2001) (ed.) *The Blackwell Guide to Philosophical Logic* (Oxford: Blackwell).

Gödel, Kurt

(1933) "Eine Interpretation des intuitionistischen Aussagenkalkuls" ["An Interpretation of Intuitionistic propositional Calculus"], *Ergebnisse eines mathematisches Kolloquiums* 4: 39–40, reprinted with

References

English trans. by J. Dawson in S. Feferman et al., eds., *Collected Works of Kurt Gödel*, vol. 1: *Publications 1929–1936* (Oxford: Oxford University Press), 300–303.

Goldblatt, Robert

(1980) "Diodorean Modality in Minkowski Spacetime," *Studia Logica* 39: 219–36.

(2006) "Mathematical Modal Logic: A View of Its Evolution," *Journal of Applied Logic* 1: 309–92.

Hailperin, Theodore

(1996) *Sentential Probability Logic: Origins, Development, Current Status, and Technical Applications* (Bethlehem, PA: Lehigh University Press).

Harrel, David

(1984) "Dynamic Logic," in (Gabbay & Guenthner, 1984), 497–604.

Heyting, Arend

(1956) *Intuitionism* (Amsterdam: North Holland).

Kripke, Saul

(1963) "Semantical Considerations on Modal Logic," *Acta Philosophical Fennica* 16: 83–94.

Lewis, Clarence I., and Cooper H. Langford

(1932) *Symbolic Logic* (New York: Century).

Lewis, David

(1986) *Counterfactuals*, revised reprinting (Cambridge, MA: Harvard University Press).

Neale, Stephen

(2000) "On a Milestone of Empiricism," in P. Kotatko and A. Orenstein, eds., *Knowledge, Language and Logic: Questions for Quine* (Dordrecht: Kluwer), 237–346.

Palmer, Frank R.

(1986) *Mood and Modality*, 2nd ed. (Cambridge: Cambridge Textbooks in Linguistics, Cambridge University Press).

Pnueli, Amir

(1977) "The Temporal Logic of Programs," *Proceedings of the 18th IEEE Symposium on the Foundations of Computer Science*, 46–67.

Prawitz, Dag

(1977) "Meaning and Proofs: The Conflict between Classical and Intuitionistic Logic," *Theoria* (Lund) 43: 2–43.

Priest, Graham

    (2006) *In Contradiction*, 2nd ed. (Oxford: Oxford University Press).

Prior, Arthur N.

    (1967) *Past, Present and Future* (Oxford: Clarendon Press).

Quine, Willard van Orman

    (1953) "Reference and Modality," in *From a Logical Point of View*, 1st ed. (Cambridge, MA: Harvard University Press).

Restall, Gregory

    (2000) *An Introduction to Substructural Logics* (London: Routledge).

Shapiro, Stewart

    (2005) (ed.) *The Oxford Handbook of Philosophy of Mathematics and Logic* (Oxford: Oxford University Press).

Tennant, Neil

    (1997) *The Taming of the True* (Oxford: Oxford University Press).

Thomason, Richmond

    (1984) "Combinations of Tense and Modality," in (Gabbay & Guenthner, 1984), 135–65.

Index

Index

decidability: of classical monadic predicate logic, 138; of classical sentential logic, 5–6; of intuitionistic sentential logic, 130; of modal and temporal logics, 61–62

deducibility, 11, 132

deductions, 114–117; conditional, 85–87

deduction theorems, 115, 117–118

deductive closure, 56, 132

demonstrability, 11; as a modality, 46, 64–65

denotation function of a model, 8

density, 27

descriptive *vs* prescriptive logic, 2, 120

dialethism, 112–113, 120

disjunction (∨), 3; intensional (+), 108–110, 120; introduction rule for, 99, 101, 102–103, 109; syllogism rule for, 99, 101, 108–110, 120

double negation interpretation of intuitionistic logic, 127–130

duality, rule of, 24–25, 49

Dummett, Michael, 121, 122–123, 125, 142

Edgington, Dorothy, 98

elections, examples pertaining to, 80–81, 93–94, 95–96

entailment, as synonymous with logical implication, 99

epistemic "will" and "may," 97

error theory of conditionals, 79

excluded middle, 121, 130, 140–141

existential closure, 9

extendibility, 27

Fine models, 118, 120

finite model property, 61

first-degree relevance/relevant logic, 107–108

form, logical, and formalization, 2–3, 4, 7–8

formulas, 3–4, 7; closed *vs* open, 8, 36; flat, 62–64

frames, 14, 27, 49–51

generated submodels theorem, 62

Gentzen cut elimination theorem, 106

glitches or hazards, in circuits, 112

Gödel, Kurt, 130, 141

grammaticalization, 16, 40

Grice, H. P., 98

Hájek, Alan, 98

Hamblin's theorem, 32–33

hereditary valuation, 130–131

Hesperus and Phosphorus, 68

Heyting, Arend, 141; his axiomatization, 125

hypothetical syllogism, 79–80, 84, 93, 95

I. *See* Heyting, Arend: his axiomatization

idealism, in the theory of conditionals, 78–79

identity and non-identity (= and ≠), 7; necessity of, 69; permanence of, 33, 34–35

implication, logical, 2

implicature. *See* conventional implicature; conversational implicature

inconsistency, negation *vs* absolute, 132–133

induction on complexity, 4

infinitely proceeding sequences, 139–141

intermediate logics (**KC** and **LC**), 135–136

interpolation. *See* Craig interpolation theorem

intuitionism, in mathematics, 121, 123, 138–141

intuitionistic logic, 2, 121–142

irreflexivity, 60–61

isomorphism, 10

Index